The
Princeton
Review®

CRASH COURSE for the GRE

6th Edition

The Staff of The Princeton Review

PrincetonReview.com

Penguin
Random
House

The Princeton Review
555 W. 18th Street
New York, NY 10011
E-mail: editorialsupport@review.com

Published in the United States by Random House LLC, New York, and in Canada by Random House of Canada, a division of Penguin Random House Ltd., Toronto.

Terms of Service: The Princeton Review Online Companion Tools ("Student Tools") for retail books are available for only the two most recent editions of that book. Student Tools may be activated only twice per eligible book purchased for two consecutive 12-month periods, for a total of 24 months of access. Activation of Student Tools more than twice per book is in direct violation of these Terms of Service and may result in discontinuation of access to Student Tools Services.

ISBN: 978-0-451-48784-1
eBook ISBN: 978-1-5247-1031-6
ISSN: 1545-620X

GRE is a registered trademark of Educational Testing Service, which is not affiliated with The Princeton Review.

The Princeton Review is not affiliated with Princeton University.

Editor: Orion McBean
Production Editor: Liz Rutzel
Production Artist: Deborah A. Silvestrini

Printed in the United States of America.

10 9 8 7 6 5 4 3 2 1

6th Edition

Editorial
Rob Franek, Editor-in-Chief
Casey Cornelius, VP Content Development
Mary Beth Garrick, Director of Production
Selena Coppock, Managing Editor
Meave Shelton, Senior Editor
Colleen Day, Editor
Sarah Litt, Editor
Aaron Riccio, Editor
Orion McBean, Editorial Assistant

Penguin Random House Publishing Team
Tom Russell, VP, Publisher
Alison Stoltzfus, Publishing Director
Jake Eldred, Associate Managing Editor
Ellen Reed, Production Manager
Suzanne Lee, Designer

Acknowledgments

The Princeton Review would like to thank Kyle Fox, Rachel Suvorov, Beth Hollingsworth, and Kevin Kelly for their dedication, hard work, and expertise with revising the 6th Edition.

Special thanks to Adam Robinson, who conceived of and perfected the Joe Bloggs approach to standardized tests, and many of the other successful techniques used by The Princeton Review.

Lastly, the editor of this book would like to thank Deborah A. Silvestrini, Liz Rutzel and Sara Kuperstein for their work on this edition.

Contents

Register Your

1 Go to **PrincetonReview.com/cracking**

2 You'll see a welcome page where you can register your book using the following ISBN: 9780451487841

3 After placing this free order, you'll either be asked to log in or to answer a few simple questions in order to set up a new Princeton Review account.

4 Finally, click on the "Student Tools" tab located at the top of the screen. It may take an hour or two for your registration to go through, but after that, you're good to go.

If you have noticed potential content errors, please contact **EditorialSupport@review.com** with the full title of the book, its ISBN number (located above), and the page number of the error.

Experiencing technical issues? Please e-mail **TPRStudentTech@review.com** with the following information:

- your full name
- e-mail address used to register the book
- full book title and ISBN
- your computer OS (Mac or PC) and Internet browser (Firefox, Safari, Chrome, etc.)
- description of technical issue

Book Online!

Once you've registered, you can...

- Plan your review sessions with study plans based on your schedule—1 week, 2 weeks, or 4 weeks

- Print and memorize GRE key terms and work through vocabulary matching exercises

- Read important advice about the GRE and graduate school

- Access crucial information about the graduate school application process, including a timeline and checklist

- Check to see if there have been any corrections or updates to this edition

Offline Resources

- *Verbal Workout for the GRE, 6th Edition*

- *Math Workout for the GRE, 4th Edition*

- *1,007 GRE Practice Questions, 4th Edition*

PART I
Orientation

Introduction

What Is *Crash Course for the GRE*?

Crash Course for the GRE is a quick but thorough guide to the fundamentals of the GRE. It includes helpful techniques for nailing as many questions as possible, even if you don't have a lot of time to prepare. *Crash Course for the GRE* will give you an overview of the test, exposure to all question types, and loads of helpful advice, including 10 specific tips on how to improve your score. But remember that this book is *not* intended to be a comprehensive study guide for the GRE. If you need significant score improvements or a more intensive review of any of the subject matter you encounter, try our other helpful GRE books, *Cracking the GRE, 1,007 GRE Practice Questions, Math Workout for the GRE,* or *Verbal Workout for the GRE*. You can also register to take a free full-length GRE practice test online at **PrincetonReview.com/grad/gre-practice-test**.

What Is the GRE?

The Graduate Record Exam (GRE) is a 3-hour and 45-minute exam intended to rank applicants for graduate schools. It does not measure your intelligence, nor is it a realistic measure of how well you'll do in graduate school. It is safe to say the GRE provides a valid assessment of only one thing: how well you take the GRE. Luckily, this is a skill you can improve with practice.

After you take the GRE, you will receive a Analytical Writing score, a Verbal Reasoning score, and a Quantitative Reasoning score. These correspond to the three types of sections you will see on the test.

Section by section, here's how the test breaks down:

Section	Number of Questions	Allotted Time
Analytical Writing (one section with two separately timed essays)	One "Analyze an Issue" essay and one "Analyze an Argument" essay	30 minutes per essay
Verbal Reasoning (two sections)	20 questions per section	30 minutes per section
Quantitative Reasoning (two sections)	20 questions per section	35 minutes per section
Break	—	10 minutes
Experimental/ Unscored	Varies	Varies
Research	Varies	Varies

The Analytical Writing, or essay section, always comes first. It consists of two back-to-back essays, with 30 minutes each to write. After the essays, you will have two of your five multiple-choice sections, and then you will get your one and only proper break after the third section. Most students see five multi-question sections, either two Verbal and three Quantitative (Math), or three Verbal and two Math. Two Verbal sections and two Math sections always count. The extra section is an experimental one. It may be Math or Verbal. It will look just like the other sections, but it will not count. These five sections, including the experimental, could occur in any order. There is no way to know which section is experimental. You will have a one-minute break between each of these sections.

You might also get a research section in place of the experimental section. If so, the research section will come last, and it will be identified as a research section. The test will specifically say that the section does not count toward your score. If you see one of these, your test is over, and your first four multi-question sections counted.

Math Question Types

Quantitative Comparison—Quant comps, for short, give you information in two columns. Your job is to decide if the values in the two columns are the same, if one is greater, or if it is impossible to determine.

Problem Solving—These are the typical multiple-choice questions that are common on standardized tests such as the SAT. You must correctly select one of the five answer choices to get credit.

Select All That Apply—This question type is similar to a standard multiple-choice question but with one twist. In this case there are three to eight answer choices, and one or more is correct. You must select all of the correct answer choices to get credit.

Numeric Entry—Alas, these are not multiple choice. It is your job to come up with your own answer and type it into the box provided. For fractions, you are given two boxes, and you must fill in the top and the bottom boxes separately. You don't have to reduce fractions. The computer reads $\frac{44}{88}$ the same as $\frac{1}{2}$, so save yourself a step.

The Calculator

The computer-delivered GRE provides an on-screen calculator. This calculator will add, subtract, multiply, divide, and find a square root, plus have a decimal function and a positive/negative feature. It also has a transfer number button that allows you to transfer the number on the calculator screen directly to the answer box for Numeric Entry questions. This button will be grayed out for multiple-choice questions.

The calculator can help you cut down on basic calculation errors and save a bit of time on questions that involve things like averages or percentages. The GRE, however, is not generally a test of your ability to do large calculations; nor is the calculator a replacement for your brain. The test makers will look for ways to test your analytical skills, often making the calculator an unnecessary temptation, or, at times, even a liability. Be particularly careful of questions that ask you to provide answers in a specific format. A question may ask you to provide an answer rounded to the nearest tenth, for example. If your calculator gives you an answer of 3.48, and you transfer that number, you will get the question wrong. Or a question may ask you for a percent and will have the percent symbol next to the answer box. In this case they are looking for a whole number. Depending upon how you solve the problem on your calculator, you may end up with an answer of 0.25 for 25 percent. If you enter the decimal, you will get the question wrong.

Here are a few tips for when to use and when not to use your calculator on the GRE:

Use a Calculator When...

- multiplying two- and three-digit numbers

- finding percentages or averages

- working questions involving Order of Operations (The calculator will follow the Order of Operations. If you type in $3 + 5 \times 6$, it will know to prioritize multiplication over addition, for example.)

- working with decimals

Do NOT Use a Calculator When...

- converting fractions to decimals in order to avoid working with fractions (better that you know the rules and are comfortable with fractions)

- attempting to solve great exponents, square roots, or other calculation-heavy operations. There is almost always a faster way to do the problem.

- adding or subtracting negative numbers if you're not sure of the rules

Verbal Question Types

Text Completion—Questions may have between one and five sentences and one to three blanks. A one-blank question will have five answer choices. A two- or three-blank question will have three choices per blank. You must select the correct word for each blank to get credit for the question.

Sentence Equivalence—These have one blank and six answer choices. You must select two answer choices from the six provided. The correct answers will complete the sentence and keep the meaning the same.

Reading Comprehension—Reading Comp supplies you with a passage and then asks you questions about the information in the passage, the author's intent, or the structure.

There are three distinct question types in the Verbal sections:

- **Multiple Choice**—You must select one correct answer from five choices.

- **Select All That Apply**—These have three answer choices. You must select all that are correct to receive credit. At least one choice is correct.

- **Select in Passage**—You will be asked to click on an actual sentence in the passage. You may click on any one word to select the whole sentence. Only one sentence is correct. These questions will occur primarily on short passages. If they occur for a long passage, the question will specify a particular paragraph.

What Does a GRE Score Look Like?

You will receive separate Verbal and Quantitative scores, each on a scale that runs from 130 to 170 in one-point increments. Your Analytical Writing score is on a scale of 0 to 6 in half-point increments. For example:

YOUR SCORES:

163 QUANT

158 VERBAL

5.5 ANALYTIC

Before you see your scores, you will be given the opportunity to cancel them. If you choose not to cancel, you can make use of the GRE *ScoreSelect*® service, allowing you to select which score you want to send to schools. Options for sending scores depend on whether you are sending them on the day of your test or after your test day. For more information on this service, visit **www.ets. org/gre/revised_general/about/scoreselect.**

Who is ETS?

The GRE is created and administered by Educational Testing Service, (ETS), under the sponsorship of the Graduate Record Examinations Board, an organization affiliated with the Association of Graduate Schools and the Council of Graduate Schools in the United States.

ETS is also the organization that brings you the SAT, the Test of English as Foreign Language (TOEFL), the National Teacher Examination (NTE), and licensing and certification exams in dozen of fields.

Why Should I Listen to The Princeton Review?

We monitor the GRE. Our teaching methods for cracking it were developed through exhaustive analysis of all available GRE tests and careful research into the methods by which standardized tests are constructed. Our focus is on the basic concepts that will enable you to attack any problem, strip it down to its essential components, and solve it in as little time as possible.

GRE Facts

The GRE test fee is $205. You can register to take your test online or by phone. To register online, you need to create or have an ETS Account. Go to **www.ets.org/gre** and click on "Register for the Test" under "General Test" to create an online account. If you are registering by phone, call the test center directly at (800) 473-2255 at least two business days before your anticipated test date. ETS accepts all major credit cards.

ETS' website will answer most questions, including registering for the paper-based GRE test, guidelines for disability accommodations and international testing, as well as test center locations and dates. For additional questions, visit **www.ets.org/gre** or call ETS at (609) 771-7670.

What the GRE Looks Like

On the computer-delivered GRE, the problem you're working on will be in the middle of the screen. If there is additional information, such as a chart or graph or passage, it will be on a split screen either above the question or to the left of it. If the entire chart(s) or passage or additional information does not fit on the split screen, there will be a scroll bar.

Questions with only a single answer will have an oval selection field. To select an answer, just click on the oval. A question with the potential for multiple correct answers will have square answer fields. An **x** appears in the square when you select the answer choice. At the bottom of the screen, under the question, there may be some basic directions, such as "Click on your choice."

A read-out of the time remaining in the section will be displayed in the upper-right corner. Next to it is a button that allows you to hide the time. The time is always displayed and blinks on and off when you have five minutes remaining in a section. The top center of the screen shows which question number you are working on, out of the total number of questions. The top of the screen will also contain the following five buttons.

Exit Section—This button indicates that you are done with a particular section. Should you finish a section early, you can use this button to get to the next section. Once you've exited a section, however, you cannot return to it. Note that the two essays are considered a single section. If you use this button after your first essay, you will have skipped the second essay.

Review—This button brings up a review screen. The review screen indicates which questions you've seen, which ones you've answered, and which ones you've marked. From the review screen you can return to the question you've just left, or you can return to an earlier question.

Mark—The Mark button is just what it looks like. You can mark a question for whatever reason you choose. Marking a question does not answer the question. You can mark a question whether you've answered it or not. Marked questions appear as marked on the review screen.

Help—The Help button drops you into the Help tab for the particular question type you are working on. From there, there are three additional tabs. One gives you "Section Directions." This is an overview of the section, including the number of questions, the amount of time allotted, and a brief description of the function of ovals versus boxes. The second is "General Directions" on timing and breaks, test information, and the repeater policy. The last additional tab is "Testing Tools." This is an overview of each of the buttons available to you during a section. Note that the Help button will not stop the clock. The clock continues to run even if you are clicking around and reading directions.

Back/Next—These two buttons take you to the next question or back to the prior question. You can continue to click these as many times as you like until you get to the beginning or end of the section. If you return to a question you have answered, the question will display your answer.

We will talk more about strategies for pacing on the test and ways to use the Mark and Review buttons. You should never need the Help button. Ideally you will be familiar enough with the functions of the test that you don't have to spend valuable test time reading directions.

**You should never need the Help button.
Be familiar with the testing
tools before you go into the test.**

How the GRE Works

The GRE is adaptive by section. Your score is determined by the number of questions you get correct and their difficulty level. On the first Verbal section, the test gives you a mix of mostly medium questions along with a few easy and hard questions. Based upon the number of questions you get correct on that first section, the computer selects the difficulty of your second section. Your goal is to get as many questions correct in the first section as possible. If you get enough questions correct in the first section, your second section will be hard, but you'll also have a chance of getting the highest possible score. If you get too many questions incorrect in the first section, your second section will be easier, but there will also be a cap on how high your score can be.

Additional Resources

You bought *Crash Course for the GRE* because you want the basics and probably don't have a lot of time to prepare. Although this book is a great way to prepare for the GRE in a limited amount of time, you still need real GRE questions on which to practice. The only source of real GREs is the publisher of the test, ETS. Therefore, if you have the time, we recommend that you download GRE *POWERPREP® II*, Version 2.2 software from **www.ets.org/gre.** This software includes two complete GRE practice tests. You can also download the PDF *Practice Book for the Paper-based GRE® revised General Test, 2nd Edition.* While the format of the paper-based test is different from the computer-based test, the practice questions contained in the PDF are relevant and useful. Both of these helpful resources are mentioned in the study plans online, so it is highly recommended that you use them in addition to this book.

Stay Up To Date

The information in this book is accurate up to the time of publication. For the most current information possible, visit **www.ets.org/gre** or our website at **PrincetonReview.com.**

General Strategy

Take on the Easy Question First!

The types of questions on the GRE vary in difficulty. Some are a breeze, while others will have you pulling your hair out. The GRE is designed so that you can answer questions in any order you like within a given section, and the difficulty of the questions you get on the second section depends upon the number of questions you get correct on the first section. You can maximize that number by starting with the questions you find the easiest. Remember that every question counts equally toward your score. As you work through a section, if you encounter a question you find difficult, skip it. If you see one that looks as if it will take a long time, skip it. If you love geometry but hate algebra, do all of the geometry questions first and leave the algebra questions for last.

Unless you are shooting for a 165 or higher, you should NOT attempt to work on every single question.

If you are going to run out of time, you might as well run out of time on the questions you are least likely to get correct. By leaving time-consuming and difficult questions until the end, you will be able to see more questions overall and get more of them correct. Do not mark questions you skip; we will use the Mark function for something else. Just click "Next" and move on to the next question. The review screen will tell you which questions you have and have not answered.

Note: There is no guessing penalty on the GRE. They don't take points away for a wrong answer. When you get to the two-minute mark, therefore, stop what you're doing and just select a random letter for the unanswered questions.

Answer Questions in Stages

Any time you practice for a test, you end up getting a few questions wrong. Later, when reviewing these questions, you end up smacking your forehead and asking yourself, "What was I thinking?" Or, you may find a problem utterly impossible to solve the first time around, only to look at it later and realize that it was actually quite easy; you just misread the question or missed a key piece of information.

On an approximately four-hour test, your brain is going to get tired. When your brain gets tired, you're more likely to make mistakes. Typically these mistakes consist of misreadings or simple calculation errors. A misread question or a calculation error completely changes the way you see the problem. Unfortunately, once you see a question wrong, it is almost impossible to see it correctly. As long as you stay with that question, you will continue to see it wrong every time. Meanwhile, the clock is ticking and you're not getting any closer to the answer.

On the flip side, once you've spotted the error, solving the problem correctly is often quick work. A question that bedeviled you for minutes in the middle of a test may appear to be appallingly obvious when viewed in the comfort of a post-test review. The trick is to change the way you see the question while you still have the opportunity to fix it. Remember the following three stages to handling difficult questions.

Stage 1—Recognize that you're stuck.

Stage 2—Distract your brain.

Stage 3—See the problem with fresh eyes and fix it.

Stage 1—Recognize that you're stuck. This is often the hardest part of the process. The more work you've put into a problem, the more difficult it is to walk away from it. Once you get off track on a problem, however, any additional work you invest in that same question is wasted. If you understand what's being asked, none of the questions on the GRE should ever take more than a few minutes to solve. If you go over three minutes, you're stuck. Move on. If you find yourself working too hard, or plowing through reams of calculations, you are off track. Move on. Here are a few signs that you're stuck and need to move on:

- you've found an answer, but it is not one of the choices they've given you

- you have half a page of calculations but are no closer to an answer

- you've spent more than three minutes on a problem

- your hand is not moving

- you're down to two answer choices, and you are convinced that both are correct

- you're beginning to wonder if they made a mistake when they wrote the question

If you find yourself in any of these situations, you are definitely stuck and need to move on. You've got better things to do with your time than sit around wrestling with one question.

Stage 2—Distract your brain. Think of it this way: You could spend more than three minutes on a question even when you know you're stuck, or you could walk away and spend those same minutes on two or three other easier questions and get them all correct. Why throw good minutes after bad? Whether they realize it or not, ETS has actually designed the test to facilitate this process. This is where the Mark button comes into play. If you don't like a problem or don't know how to solve it, just skip it. If you start a problem and get stuck, mark it and move to the next question before you waste too much time. Do two or three other problems and then return to the problem that was giving you trouble.

When you "walk away" from a problem, you're not walking away entirely; you're just moving it to the back burner. Your brain is still chewing on it, but it's processing in the background while you work on something else. Sometimes your best insights occur when your attention is pointed elsewhere. Don't be afraid to walk away from a problem and return to it later. It's even okay to take two or three runs at a hard problem.

Stage 3—See the problem with fresh eyes and fix it. You use other problems to distract your brain so that when you return you can see a troublesome problem with fresh eyes. You can help this process by reading the question differently when you return to it. Use your finger on the screen to force yourself to read the problem word for word. Are there different ways to express the information? Can you use the answer choices to help? Can you paraphrase the answer choices as well? If the path to the correct answer is not clear on a second viewing, walk away again. Why stick with a problem you don't know how to solve?

The Power of POE

There are roughly four times as many wrong answers as there are correct answers; it's often easier to identify the wrong answers than it is to identify the right ones. POE stands for Process of Elimination. On difficult questions, spend your time looking for and eliminating wrong answers. They are easier and quicker to find.

The simple act of eliminating wrong answers will raise your score. Why? Because every time you're able to eliminate an incorrect choice on a GRE question, you improve your odds of finding the answer. The more incorrect choices you eliminate, the better your odds. Don't be afraid to arrive at the correct answer indirectly. You'll be avoiding the traps laid in your path by the test writers—traps that are designed to catch unwary test takers who try to approach the problems directly.

If you guessed blindly on a five-choice GRE problem, you would have one chance in five of picking ETS's answer. Eliminate one incorrect choice, and your chances improve to one in four. Eliminate three, and you have a fifty-fifty chance of earning points by guessing. Eliminating answer choices improves your odds of getting the question correct!

Note: Especially on Verbal questions, if you're not sure what a word in an answer choice means, don't eliminate that choice. It might be the answer! Eliminate only the answers you know are wrong.

The "Best" Answer

The instructions on the GRE tell you to select the "best" answer to each question. ETS calls them "best" answers, or the "credited responses," instead of "correct" answers, to protect itself from the complaints of test takers who might be tempted to quarrel with ETS's judgment. You have to pick from the choices ETS gives you, and sometimes you might not like any of them. Your job is to find the one answer for which ETS gives credit.

Use Your Scratch Paper!

For POE to work, it's crucial that you keep track of which choices you're eliminating. By crossing out a clearly incorrect choice, you permanently eliminate it from consideration. If you don't cross it out, you'll keep considering it. Crossing out incorrect choices can make it much easier to find the credited response because there will be fewer places where it can hide. But how can you cross anything out on a computer screen?

By using your scratch paper! On the GRE, the answer choices have empty bubbles next to them, but in this book, we'll refer to them as (A), (B), (C), (D), and (E). Each time you see a question, get in the habit of immediately writing down A, B, C, D, E on your scratch paper. By the time you've done a few questions, your scratch paper will be organized like this:

A	A	A	A
B	B	B	B
C	C	C	C
D	D	D	D
E	E	E	E
A	A	A	A
B	B	B	B
C	C	C	C
D	D	D	D
E	E	E	E

Then you can physically cross out choices that you eliminate. Do it every time you work through a GRE question, whether in this book or elsewhere. Get used to writing on scratch paper instead of near the question, because you won't be able to write near the question on test day.

Don't Do Anything in Your Head

Besides eliminating incorrect answers, there are many other ways to use scratch paper to solve questions; you're going to learn them all. Just remember: Even if you're tempted to try to solve questions in your head, even if you think that writing things down on your scratch paper is a waste of time, you're wrong. Trust us. Always write everything down.

Read and Copy Carefully

You can do all the calculations right and still get a question wrong. How? What if you solve for x but the question was "What is the value of $x + 3$?" Because of this, always reread the question. Take your time and don't be careless. The question will stay on the screen; it's not going anywhere.

Or, how about this? The radius of the circle is 6, but when you copied the picture onto your scratch paper, you accidentally labeled the radius 5! Many of the mistakes you make at first might stem from copying information down incorrectly. Learn from your mistakes and be extra careful when copying down information.

Accuracy Versus Speed

You don't get points for speed; the only thing that matters is accuracy. Take the time to work through each problem carefully (as long as you leave some time at the end of the section to select an answer for any question you didn't work on). If you're making careless errors, you won't even realize you're getting questions wrong. Get into the habit of double-checking all of your answers before you choose them. However, don't spend too much time on a question. When you get stuck, mark the question, move on, and return after you've answered a few other questions.

At the Testing Center

When going to take your test, you are encouraged to bring two forms of identification; one must be a recent photo ID and have your signature. Acceptable ID documents depend on where you're taking your test, so we recommend you confirm your documentation on the ETS website before your test day.

Then when your identification is verified, a test administrator will take your photo before taking you to the computer station where you will take the test. You get a desk, a computer, a keyboard, a mouse, about six pieces of scratch paper, and two pencils. Before the test begins, make sure your desk is sturdy and you have enough light, and don't be afraid to speak up if you want to move.

If there are other people in the room, they might not be taking the GRE. They could be taking a nursing test or a licensing exam for architects. And they will not necessarily have started their exams at the same time. The testing center employee will get you set up at your computer, but from then on, the computer itself will act as your proctor. It'll tell you how much time you have left in a section, when time is up, and when to move on to the next section.

The test center administrators will be monitoring the testing room for security purposes with closed-circuit television. If you have a question, or need to request extra scratch paper during the test, try to do so between the timed sections or during your break.

Let Past Questions Go

When you begin a new section, focus on that section and put the last one behind you. Don't think about that pesky text completion question from an earlier section while a geometry question is on your screen. You can't go back, and besides, your impression of how you did on a section is probably much worse than reality.

At the End of the Test

When you're done with the test, the computer will ask you twice if you want this test to count. If you select "no," the computer will not record your score, no schools will see it, and you won't see it either. You can't look at your score and then decide whether you want to keep it or not. Once your score is canceled, it can not be retrieved. If you choose to keep your scores, the computer will give you your unofficial Verbal and Quantitative scores right there on the screen. A few weeks later, your official scores will be available in your ETS account and will include your analytical score.

Test Day Checklist

- Dress in layers so that you'll be comfortable regardless of whether the room is cool or warm.

- Be sure to have breakfast or lunch, depending on the time for which your test is scheduled. And go easy on the liquids and caffeine.

- Do a few GRE practice problems to warm up your brain. Don't try to tackle difficult new questions, but review a few questions that you've done before to help you review the problem-solving strategies for each section of the GRE. This will also help you put your "game face" on and get you into test mode.

- Make sure to bring two forms of identification (one with a recent photograph and your signature) to the test center. Acceptable forms of identification generally include driver's licenses, State and Military IDs and valid passports. Check the ETS website to confirm your country's ID requirements before test day.

PART II

Ten Steps to Scoring Higher on the GRE

Use Scratch Paper for
Verbal Questions

STEP 1

Use Scratch Paper for Verbal Questions

Use Scratch Paper for Verbal Questions

For the Verbal Reasoning Section of the GRE, most people answer the Text Completion and Sentence Equivalent questions in their heads. This is not a good idea! When you answer these types of questions in your head, you are really doing two things at once. The first is evaluating each answer choice, one by one, and the second is keeping track of which answer choices are in and which are out. Studies show that multitasking cannot be done very well. The brain is simply not equipped to do too many things correctly and efficiently at once. What most people call multitasking is really jumping back and forth between multiple tasks. People who attempt to multitask inevitably end up doing both tasks poorly. People who try to multitask make more mistakes because they are constantly distracting their brains from the task at hand. Therefore, try not to multitask and do Text Completion or Sentence Equivalence questions in your head. It leads to careless and avoidable mistakes that could be catastrophic to your score.

The solution is to *engage with the question.* This means using scratch paper. Scratch paper is as important on the Verbal portion of the test as it is on the Math portion of the test. If your hand is not moving, you are stuck thinking. Thinking does not get you any closer to the answer. You should be doing, not thinking, while taking the GRE.

Here is what your scratch paper for Text Completion and Sentence Equivalence questions could look like:

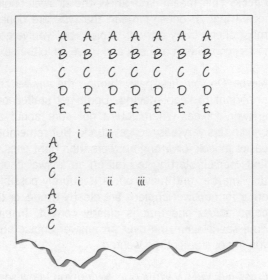

Scratch paper allows you to park your thinking on paper. On the Verbal section of the test, it's very possible that there will be words or answers you don't know. Looking for the correct answer, therefore, will work only part of the time. Fortunately, the majority of the Verbal section is multiple choice. They've actually given you the answers, and one of those answers is correct. If you can't identify the correct answer, you can always identify some wrong ones. You're probably doing this already; you're just not capturing the results on the page.

Once you start parking your thoughts on paper, however, a few good things happen. The first is that you avoid redundant work. Once you eliminate an answer choice, it's gone. You don't have to look at it again. Next, you save time because you aren't going back over ground you've already covered. And the last benefit is that you save yourself a lot of mental effort. It's hard keeping track of decisions in your head. During a four-hour test, your brain is going to get tired. Saving mental effort makes a difference.

Use these symbols on your scratch paper to capture your progress:

✔ **Check:** This means you know the answer choice, and it looks right. It doesn't mean that you are done. You still must check every answer choice, but you've got one that looks good. Give it a check and move on to the next one.

~ **Maybe:** On your first pass through the answer choices, it's important to keep moving. Don't get stalled on a single answer choice. When you're not sure about an answer choice, it's very easy to get stuck. But remember that it's easier to look for wrong answers than right ones. So, if you find yourself starting to stall on an answer choice, give it the "maybe" and move on. It is entirely possible that the other four answer choices are clearly wrong, or that you've come across one that is clearly correct. In either case, time spent agonizing over an answer choice about which you're not sure is time wasted.

A **Cross-out:** We love this one. When you know something is wrong, get rid of it. You never want to spend time on that answer choice ever again. Even if you have to guess, you want to guess from as few answer choices as possible. There are about four times as many wrong answers on the GRE as there are right ones. The wrong ones are much easier to find. Identify them and eliminate them. Keep track with your hand.

? **Question Mark:** If you don't know a word, don't eliminate it. Be honest with yourself. If you don't like the word, you don't have to pick it, but don't be quick to eliminate it because it can possibly be the answer. If you're unsure of a word, give it a question mark and move on to the next answer choice.

In all cases, the place to invest your time is in the question stem and in coming up with your own answer. The answer choices are designed to tempt and mislead you. By the time you get to the answer choices, your first pass through should be fairly quick. Either you know the word or answer choice and it works, you know it and it doesn't work, or you don't know it. If you find yourself starting to stall, give the answer a "maybe" and move on. But don't use the "maybe" as a way of avoiding making a decision!

With your evaluations marked on the page, your scratch paper can often answer the question for you. Consider these five common scenarios:

1. A, B, C, ~, E If you have an answer choice and it works, go with it. Look at this scratch paper. Your decision is made.

2. A̶, B̶, C̶, ?, E̶ What more do you need to know? You have four wrong answers and one you don't know. If the other four are wrong, they're wrong. You have no choice. There is only one possible answer choice.

3. A̶, ~, C̶, ~, E̶ If you need to spend more time on an answer choice, you always can, but don't do it until you have to. In this case, you're down to two. Do what you can to inform your guess, but don't go crazy. Pick one and move on or skip and come back.

4. A̶, B̶, C̶, D̶, E̶ You've eliminated all five. Something's gone wrong. Most likely, you've misread something in the question or something in the answer choices. You'll never see your mistake unless you distract your brain. Mark the question, move on, and come back after you've done a few others.

5. A̶, ?, C̶, ?, E̶ You're down to two. You don't know the words. You've eliminated all that you can. Don't spend any more time. Pick an answer and move on.

Using scratch paper with these types of questions is a good habit. Start practicing now and force yourself to use it. The more you use it, the more it will ease your decision making. Eventually, you won't be able to do it any other way. This is the goal. It's hard work at first, but good techniques should become automatic with enough practice.

STEP 2

Slow Down for Reading Comprehension

Slow Down for Reading Comprehension

For the Reading Comprehension questions of the Verbal Reasoning section, the answers are in the passages given to you. There are three ways you can give yourself more time on Reading Comprehension questions:

- The first way is to get so good at Text Completions and Sentence Equivalence that you have plenty of time left over for Reading Comp, where time equals points.

- The second way to pick up time is to pick your battles. Take on fewer passages, do fewer questions, but get more correct. Rushing through Reading Comp guarantees wrong answers. Slow down and make sure that the time you spend yields points.

- The last way to give yourself more time on Reading Comp is to be smart about where you spend your time. There is a lot of information in the passages, but you will be tested on only a tiny portion of that information. A smart and efficient strategy for working with the passages will pay dividends in the form of more time and less stress.

The Passages

If you are like many students, Reading Comprehension passages on the GRE are not something you'd read for fun on a Saturday afternoon. There is no way around the simple fact that most GRE Reading Comprehension passages are mundane in content and tedious in structure. While it is true that the passages are, for the most part, boring, the good news is that all the questions can be answered by the information presented in the text. Most of the Reading Comprehension passages you'll see on the GRE are only one paragraph long, but one or two passages are several paragraphs long. You'll typically see ten passages, each of which will be followed by one to six questions. The topics covered include physical sciences, biological sciences, social sciences, business, and humanities, but no specialized knowledge of any of these fields is necessary.

The Basic Approach to Reading Comprehension

To successfully answer Reading Comprehension questions on the GRE, it is important to gain a good understanding of the passage, the question, and the answer choices. By doing so, you will be able to grasp the meaning of the passage, locate information to answer questions quickly and efficiently, and spot incorrect answers. The Basic Approach is a four-step process that will help you feel confident in your abilities to handle any GRE Reading Comprehension passage.

Here are the steps of the Basic Approach.

Step 1: Work the Passage

Working the passage is the first step toward successfully approaching GRE Reading Comprehension questions. Many students will see a Reading Comprehension question and skip straight to the question. Others will read the passage, but do so as quickly as they can so they can start working through the question. If you have found yourself doing either of these things, you're not alone. However, these strategies are not efficient because they can lead to time wasted rereading sentences, pulling information out of context, or inaccurately answering the questions.

Working the passage appropriately enables you to avoid many of those mistakes so, by the time you're finished reading, you will have a clear understanding of the passage to apply to the questions. You should work through the passage by identifying the main idea, the structure, and the author's viewpoint.

To work the passage, separate each sentence individually into one of three categories: *claim, evidence/objections*, and *background*.

- *Claims* are sentences in the passage that give you some insight as to the main point of the passage or the author's viewpoint. Most GRE authors have a point of view. However, most GRE authors are academics who express their point of view in tentative ways. If the sentence gives you any insight into what the author thinks or is trying to convince you of, it is a claim.

- *Evidence/objections* are sentences in the passage that provide information that support or argue with the claims in the passage.

- *Background* sentences provide information about the topic of discussions. Background sentences typically provide context for the discussion so that the reader has a better understanding of why the author is writing the passage in the first place.

When you work the passage, assign each sentence in the passage one of the categories and write it down on your scratch paper so it's easy to keep track. By assigning each sentence a category, you will easily be able to identify the main point and structure of the passage, as well as the author's viewpoint.

Step 2: Understand the Question

After working the passage, it's time to take a look at the question. This step might seem a little obvious to you. Of course, you need to understand the question. But, breaking the question down into its main components allows you to focus on the information in the passage you'll need to answer the question. The main components of the question are the subject and the task.

Every question has a subject and a task. The subject of the question is the topic of the question. If you identify the subject of the question, then you will know the information from the passage you need to find.

The task of the question is what information the question is asking you to find in the passage about the subject. Understanding the task will help you evaluate the information you find about the subject.

Check out the following question stem:

> It can be inferred that the author of
> the passage would most likely agree
> with which of the following claims
> about the organizers of the Haymarket
> protest?

Now, find the subject and the task of the question. The subject of the question is the topic that the question is asking about. Therefore, the subject is *the organizers of the Haymarket protest*. The task of the question is the information about the subject that will answer the question. The task is *the author of the passage would most likely agree with*.

Look at another question:

> The passage is primarily concerned
> with discussing which of the following?

The subject of the question is *the passage*. The subject is general, as it is about the entire passage, so look for the task to provide some context about how to answer the question. The task is *primarily concerned with discussing*. Therefore, you know that the answer to the question will be the main idea of the passage.

Step 3: Find the Information in the Passage That Addresses the Task of the Question

Now that you have worked the passage and you understand the question, it's time to find the information in the passage that addresses the task of the question. Find and read a couple of sentences before and after the portion of the passage that discusses the subject.

All of the questions for the GRE must be answerable based on the information in the passage. If ETS wrote a question that was not answerable based on the information in the passage, they would have no way to justify their choices and would be subject to challenges and lawsuits from disgruntled students. With that in mind, the information to answer the question can always be found in the passage. All you have to do is find it.

This is part of what makes successfully completing Step 1 so important. If you've created a good outline of the passage following those guidelines, you may not have to return to actually reading the passage. Instead, you might be able to quickly note the information based on the claims, evidence/objections, and background. At the very least, you will know where to find the information. At best, the outline will provide the appropriate information to you.

When you find the information in the passage, resist the urge to paraphrase what the passage says. Instead, use the information from the passage exactly as it is stated. If you paraphrase information, you will be susceptible to assumptions and filling in information that the author of the passage did not intend. ETS question writers expect you to do this and will write answer choices designed to trap test takers who paraphrase what the passage says. Avoid this trap and quote the passage exactly as it is stated.

Step 4: Use POE to Find the Answer

Once you've completed all the above steps, use Process of Elimination (POE) to attack the answer choices. If you successfully completed steps 1–3, you will know exactly what the passage says about the subject and task of the question. Now that you're looking at the answer choices, you'll notice that, at any given point, chances are you are reading an incorrect answer choice. After all, most of the answer choices on the GRE are wrong! Look for signs that the answer choice is incorrect, such as sounding too much like the passage or taking words from the passage out of context. Eliminate answer choices that don't match what you read about the subject in the passage, and don't be afraid to simply select the only answer choice that remains if you have a good reason to eliminate the other answer choices.

When test writers make incorrect answer choices, they use a handful of tools to make them seem appealing to test takers. These tools are designed to trick the test taker into picking certain incorrect answer choices. Having a full understanding of what the passage says about the subject and task of the question will help you to avoid these answer choices, but that is not the only method at your disposal. Being aware of the ways in which incorrect answer choices are commonly created is just as valuable.

Here are the six most common ways test writers create wrong answers.

1. Recycled Language and Memory Traps   One of the easiest and most common ways that test writers create a wrong answer choice is by repeating memorable words or phrases from the passage. The correct answers for GRE Reading Comprehension questions are generally paraphrases of the passage. Therefore, the presence of words or phrases that are very reminiscent of the passage is a reason to be skeptical of an answer choice. Any answer choice that evokes a strong memory of the passage should cause suspicion, as it could be a Recycled Language or Memory Trap answer. If you find an answer choice that feels familiar, double check to make sure the information in the passage supports the statement. If the information in the passage does not explicitly support this statement, eliminate the answer choice.

2. Extreme Language Another common way to create wrong answer choices is by using language too "powerful" or overt. Common words such as *must, always, never, only, best,* or verbs such as *prove* or *fail* are ways in which question writers make an answer choice appealing. Always compare the language in the answer against the passage to see whether the claim made is as strong as the claim in the answer choice. If the information in the passage is not as strong as the claim in the answer choice, eliminate the answer choice.

3. No Such Comparison Comparison words such as *better, more, reconcile, less, decide,* or *more than* are often used by test writers to make answer choices more appealing by drawing a comparison between two items referenced in the passage. However, these items may not have been compared in the passage. If you see comparison words in an answer choice, you should be skeptical and double check the passage. If the items being compared in the answer choice were not compared in the passage, eliminate the answer choice.

4. Reversals Reversal answer choices seek to confuse the test taker by stating the opposite of the information in the passage. Finding the appropriate information in the passage, considering the information exactly as it is phrased, and breaking down the passage to find the main idea are tools that should help you spot reversal answer choices.

5. Emotional Appeals This answer choice type is fairly rare on the GRE. However, it bears worth mentioning. Some answer choices may try to appeal to the beliefs of the test taker. For instance, a political passage may contain an answer choice that values one political stance over another even if the passage made no such claim. If you see answer choices like this, be very skeptical and refer back to the passage. You need to pick an answer based on what the passage said rather than your own beliefs about the topic.

If the passage does not support the answer choice it is wrong, no matter how much you may agree with the answer choice.

6. Outside Knowledge Like emotional appeal answer choices, outside knowledge answer choices are fairly rare on the GRE. Correct answer choices on the GRE will contain information that is found in the passage. However, some answer choices may contain information that is designed to appeal to a test taker that has some independent knowledge about the subject of the question. Remember, if the information isn't explicitly stated in the passage, it should not be considered when deciding on an answer choice.

Question Formats

Many of the questions are standard GRE fare: multiple-choice questions with five potential answers and a single correct answer. Reading Comprehension questions can also be All That Apply questions. In this case, you will be presented with three answer choices, from which you must choose one, two, or all three correct answers. Finally, there are some questions that will ask you to find the sentence in the passage that answers the question. Answer these questions by clicking on the correct sentence from the passage.

Recognize Question Types

Knowing the question type will allow you to not only quickly identify the subject and task of the question, but also be on the lookout for common wrong answer traps that are often found with certain types of questions.

There are three categories of common questions: *general, specific,* and *complex.* Each of those categories has several question types that are commonly tested on the GRE.

1. General Questions

The types of General questions are *main idea, primary purpose, tone,* and *structure.*

Main Idea questions ask you to consider the main claims made by the author. These questions generally ask what the passage is about. The answer to a Main Idea question is summarizes what the author wants you to remember about the passage. A Main Idea question can be identified by the phrase *main idea* or any reference to an overall claim.

Primary Purpose questions may seem a lot like Main Idea questions, but they differ in one important way. While Main Idea questions ask what the passage is about, Primary Purpose questions ask why the author wrote the passage. To answer a Primary Purpose question, you need to figure out why the author wrote the passage. In general, the author wrote the passage to convince you of the passage's main idea! A Primary Purpose question can be identified by the presence of the phrase *primary purpose* in the question stem.

Tone questions ask you to evaluate the author's opinion and how strongly the author feels about that opinion. Typically, the question asks about the main topic under discussion in the passage in which the author will have expressed an opinion about that topic through the main idea. Ask yourself whether the author agrees or disagrees. If you have found the main idea, deciphering the *tone* of the passage should be a manageable task. These questions are readily identifiable, as the question stem usually includes the word *tone* or *attitude.*

Structure questions ask about the overall structure of the passage, or the role of certain sentences or phrases in the passage. Each passage will have a definable structure that you should have uncovered when you worked the passage. If you worked the passage appropriately, these questions are relatively easy to answer as they will ask about the flow and content of the passage.

2. Specific Questions

The types of specific questions typically found on the GRE are *retrieval, inference, specific purpose,* and *vocabulary in context.*

Retrieval questions, which are very common, are identified by the presence of the words *according to the passage* or a similar phrase that tells you to simply find something stated in the passage. The correct answer is usually just a paraphrase of something the passage said, as Retrieval questions ask you to go back to the passage to find some fact or detail.

Inference questions are also very common on the GRE and often give test takers unaware of the question task the most trouble. These questions usually say something along the lines of *what can be inferred from the passage.* Inference questions will always be about something very specific that is stated in the passage, and because of that, are actually very similar to Retrieval questions. The answer to an Inference question is something that you know to be true based in the information in the passage. Inference questions are easily identified as they usually contain the word *infer, imply,* or *suggest* in the question.

Many students mistakenly believe Inference questions ask the reader to determine something the author thinks or believes, but does not explicitly state in the passage. This is not true. As we outlined earlier, the correct answers are always found in the passage.

Specific Purpose questions are similar to Primary Purpose questions in the sense that they both ask why the author included certain information in the passage. However, Specific Purpose questions ask about something very specific, while Primary Purpose questions are more general. These questions can be identified by phrases such as *in order to* and *serves which of the following functions.*

Vocabulary in Context questions reference a word or phrase from the passage that the author included to prove a point. The task of these questions is to determine the point or the meaning of the words of phrases indicated in the question stem.

3. Complex Questions

The complex questions are *Weaken* and *Strengthen* questions. *Weaken* and *Strengthen* questions ask the test taker to weaken or strengthen some claim in the passage. Often, the test taker must consider possible scenarios that could affect the outcome of the claim. Be on the lookout for wrong answers that accomplish the opposite task. For example, answers that weaken are common on Strengthen questions. These questions are identified by the presence of the words *weaken* or *strengthen*.

Final Thoughts

Above all, remember that the answers to Reading Comprehension questions are always found within the text. When you encounter an answer choice, always verify it with the information in the passage.

STEP 3

Cover Up the Answers for Sentence Equivalence

Cover Up the Answers for Sentence Equivalence

Directions for Sentence Equivalence questions are as follows: Select the two answer choices that, when used to complete the sentence, fit the meaning of the sentence as a whole and produce completed sentences that are alike in meaning.

In other words, figure out the story being told and pick the two words in the answer choices that complete the story in the same way. These are, in fact, Sentence Completion questions, but you are picking two words rather than one for the same blank.

The other part of Sentence Equivalence is the answer choices. They will always fit grammatically into the sentence, and quite a few of them will make a degree of sense. They represent ETS's suggestions for what to put in the blank. We don't like their suggestions, we don't trust their suggestions, and we don't want their suggestions. The answer choices have been carefully selected and then tested on thousands of students for the sole purpose of messing with your head. The first step in answering Sentence Equivalence questions is to always cover up the answer choices. Literally. Put your hand on the screen and don't let them show.

Now back to the sentence. Think of this as a mini reading comprehension passage. Before you do anything, find the main idea. Who is the passage talking about? What are you told about this person or thing? Once you have the story firmly in mind, come up with your own word for the blank, and eliminate the answer choices that don't match.

Let's try this question:

> Wilson worked _____ on his first novel, cloistering himself in his study for days on end without food or sleep.
>
> ☐ carelessly
>
> ☐ assiduously
>
> ☐ creatively
>
> ☐ tirelessly
>
> ☐ intermittently
>
> ☐ voluntarily

Step 1—Cover up the answer choices.

Step 2—Find the story. Who is the main character? Wilson. What are you told about Wilson? He's working on his first novel and has locked himself in his study for a long time without food or sleep. The dude is working hard. The blank, in fact, describes how Wilson is working.

Step 3—Come up with your own word for the blank. *Hard? Dedicated? Unceasing?*

Step 4—Use Process of Elimination (POE). Use your word to eliminate answer choices. Of each answer choice, ask yourself, "Does this word mean the same thing as or similar to _____ (my word)?" If the answer is no, get rid of it. If the answer is "I'm not sure," give it the "maybe" and move on. If the answer is yes, give it the check. All of this work takes place on your scratch paper.

(A) Does *carelessly* mean the same thing as or is it similar to *hard, dedicated,* or *unceasing?* No. Cross off (A).

(B) Does *assiduously* mean the same thing as or is it similar to *hard, dedicated,* or *unceasing?* Not sure? Give it the question mark and leave it in.

(C) Does *creatively* mean the same thing as or is it similar to *hard, dedicated,* or *unceasing?* No. Could Wilson, the first-time novelist, be working "creatively"? Sure, but it's not what you're looking for. Cross off (C).

(D) Does *tirelessly* mean the same thing as or is it similar to *hard, dedicated,* or *unceasing?* Sure does. Give it a check.

(E) Does *intermittently* mean the same thing as or is it similar to *hard, dedicated,* or *unceasing?* Nope. Cross off (E).

(F) Does *voluntarily* mean the same thing as or is it similar to *hard, dedicated,* or *unceasing?* Nope. Cross off (F).

Now look at your scratch paper. You have four no's, one yes, and one question mark. You're done. Whatever *assiduously* means, it must be similar to *hard, dedicated,* or *unceasing.* The correct answers are *tirelessly* and *assiduously.*

Finding the Clue

How did you know to put *hard, dedicated,* or *unceasing* in the blank? The sentence says, "cloistering himself in his study for days on end without food or sleep." What else could it be? That part of the sentence is what we call a clue. Every sentence will have one. Every sentence must have one because it's the part of the sentence that makes one answer correct and another one incorrect. The clue is like an arrow that points only to right answers. Finding the clue will help you to come up with your own word for the blank and will help to eliminate wrong answers. Now try the following activities.

Activity 1

In each of the following sentences, find the clue and underline it. Then, write down your own word for the blank. It doesn't matter if your guesses are awkward or wordy. All you need to do is express the correct idea.

1. Despite the apparent _____ of the demands, the negotiations dragged on for over a year.

2. Most students found Dr. Schwartz's lecture on art excessively detailed and academic; some thought his display of _____ exasperating.

Activity 2

Now look at the same questions again, this time with the answer choices provided. Use your words above to eliminate answer choices.

1. Despite the apparent _____ of the demands, the negotiations dragged on for over a year.

   ◯ hastiness
   ◯ intolerance
   ◯ publicity
   ◯ modesty
   ◯ desirability
   ◯ triviality

2. Most students found Dr. Schwartz's lecture on art excessively detailed and academic; some thought his display of _____ exasperating.

○ pedantry
○ fundamentals
○ logic
○ aesthetics
○ erudition
○ literalism

Now review the answers to Activity 2.

Question 1: The blank refers to the *demands*. The clue is *the negotiations dragged on for over a year*. The word *Despite* indicates a contrast, so a good word for the blank is something that indicates the opposite of what would be expected to cause negotiations to drag on for over a year. Therefore, a good word for the blank is something such as "smallness." Check the answer choices for a word similar to "smallness." Choice (A), *hastiness*, which means a state of being hurried, does not match "smallness." Eliminate (A). Choice (B), *intolerance*, meaning an inability to endure something, also does not match "smallness," so eliminate it. Choice (C), *publicity*, which means public attention, is not a good match for "smallness," so eliminate it as well. Choice (D), *modesty*, is a good match for smallness in this context, so keep it. Choice (E), *desirability*, meaning a state of being wanted, doesn't match smallness. Eliminate (E). Choice (F), *triviality*, matches "smallness." Keep (F). The correct answer is (D) and (F).

Question 2: The blank refers to the *display*. The clue is *Most students found Dr. Schwartz's lectures on art excessively detailed and academic*. The semicolon is a same direction transition and indicates that there isn't a contrast in the sentence. Therefore, the clue can be recycled, so "an excessively detailed and academic lecture" is a good choice for the blank. Choice (A), *pedantry*, is a good match for "an excessively detailed and academic lecture," so keep it. Choice (B), *fundamentals*, which means the basics, does not match "an excessively detailed and academic lecture." Eliminate (B). Choice (C), *logic*, meaning reason, also does not match "an excessively detailed and academic lecture," so eliminate it. Choice (D), *aesthetics*, which is the philosophy of art, does not match "an excessively detailed and academic lecture." Eliminate (D). Choice (E), *erudition*, is a good match for "an excessively detailed and academic lecture." Keep (E). Choice (F), *literalism*, meaning an exact portrayal, does not match "an excessively detailed and academic lecture," so eliminate it. The correct answer is (A) and (E).

Transition Words

Imagine a conversation that begins, "That's Frank. He won the lottery and now _____." Something good is going to go into that blank. Frank could be a millionaire, living on his own island, or a great collector of rare jeweled belt buckles. Whatever it is, this story is going to end happily.

Now consider this story: "That's Frank. He won the lottery but now _____." This story is going to end badly. Frank could be tied up in court for tax evasion, panhandling on the corner, or in a mental institution.

The only difference between these two stories is the words *but* and *and*. These are transition words.

They provide important structural indicators of the meaning of the sentence and are often the key to figuring out what words have to mean to fill in the blanks in a Sentence Completion. Some of the most important Sentence Completion transition words and punctuation are listed on the next page.

Transition Words/Punctuation	
but	in contrast
although (though, even though)	unfortunately
unless	heretofore
rather	thus
yet	and
despite	therefore
while	similarly
however	; *or* :

Paying attention to transition words is crucial to understanding the meaning of the sentence. The words from *but* to *heretofore* are "change direction" transition words, indicating that the two parts of the sentence diverge in meaning. The above words, from *thus* to the colon (:) and semicolon (;), are "same direction" transitions, indicating that the two parts of the above sentence agree. For example, if your sentence said "Judy was a fair and _____ judge," the placement of the "and" would tell you that the word in the blank would have to be similar to "fair." You could even use the word "fair" as your fill-in-the-blank word.

What if your sentence said, "Judy was a fair but _____ judge"? The placement of the "but" would tell you that the word in the blank would have to be somewhat opposite of "fair," something like "tough."

Let's try this question (we've taken the answer choices away again, for now):

Although originally created for
_____ use, the colorful,
stamped tin kitchen boxes of
the early twentieth century are
now prized primarily for their
ornamental qualities.

What's the clue in the sentence that tells you why the boxes were originally created? Well, you know that they "are now prized primarily for their ornamental qualities." Does this mean that they were originally created for "ornamental" use? No. The transition word "Although" indicates that the word for the blank will mean the opposite of "ornamental." How about "useful"? It may sound strange to say "useful use," but don't worry about how your words sound—it's what they mean that's important.

Now, here are the answer choices:

○ utilitarian
○ traditional
○ practical
○ occasional
○ annual
○ commercial

(A) Does *utilitarian* mean "useful"? Yes, give it a check on your scratch paper.

(B) Does *traditional* mean "useful"? No. Cross it off on your scratch paper.

(C) Does *practical* mean "useful"? Yes, give it a check mark.

(D) Does *occasional* mean "useful"? Nope. Get rid of it.

(E) Does *annual* mean "useful"? Nope, cross it off.

(F) Does *commercial* mean "useful"? No. Cross it off.

The answer is (A) and (C).

Positive/Negative

In some cases, you may think of several words that could go in the blanks. Or, you might not be able to think of any. Rather than spending a lot of time trying to find the "perfect" word, just ask yourself whether the missing word will be a positive word or a negative word. Then, write a + or a – symbol on your scratch paper and take it from there. Here's an example (again, without answer choices, for now):

> Trembling with anger, the belligerent colonel ordered his men to _____ the civilians.

Use those clues. You know the colonel is "Trembling with anger," and that he's "belligerent" (which means war-like). Is the missing word a "good" word or a "bad" word? It's a "bad" word. The colonel is clearly going to do something nasty to the civilians. Now go to the answer choices and eliminate any choices that are positive and, therefore, cannot be correct.

- ○ congratulate
- ○ promote
- ○ reward
- ○ attack
- ○ worship
- ○ torment

Choices (A), (B), (C), and (E) are all positive words; therefore, they can all be eliminated. The only negative words among the choices are (D) and (F), the best answers. Positive/negative won't work for every question, but sometimes it can get you out of a jam.

When it comes to Sentence Equivalence questions, remember these three things:

1. **Invest your time in the sentence.** Stick with the sentence until you find the story. You cannot go to the answer choices until that story is crystal clear.

2. **Use your word as your filter.** Come up with your own word for the blank and use it to eliminate answer choices. You should be actively identifying and eliminating wrong answers. Keep your hand moving on your scratch paper. Processing the answer choices should take no more than 20 seconds. Note: If an answer choice has no synonym among the other answer choices, it's unlikely to be correct.

3. **Mark and come back.** If a sentence isn't making sense, or none of the answer choices look correct, move on. Don't keep forcing the sentence. You may have read something wrong. Go do a few other questions to distract your brain and then take a second look at it.

Fill In the Blanks for
Text Completion Questions

STEP 4

Fill In the Blanks for Text Completion

Fill In the Blanks for Text Completion Questions

Text Completions occupy a middle ground between Sentence Equivalence and Reading Comprehension questions. You will be given a small passage—one to five sentences—with one, two, or three blanks. If the passage has one blank, you will have five answer choices. If it has two or three blanks, you will be given three answer choices per blank. You have to independently fill in each blank to get credit for the question.

The overall approach is the same. Ignore the answer choices. Find the story being told (there will always be a story), and come up with your own words for the blanks. Here's what a three-blank Text Completion will look like:

Sample Question

Directions: For each blank, select one entry from the corresponding column of choices. Fill all blanks in the way that best completes the text.

> The image of the architect as the lonely artist drawing three-dimensional forms is (i)_____ the public's understanding of the architect's role. As a result, buildings are viewed as the singular creations of an artistic vision with the artist (ii)_____ the architect. Certainly architects should take much of the credit for the form of a unique building, but the final product is hardly a (iii)_____. The architect relies heavily upon façade consultants, engineers, and skilled builders, while the form of the building may depend, in addition, upon zoning regulations, cost, and market demands.

Blank (i)	Blank (ii)	Blank (iii)
at odds with	tangentially related to	virtuoso performance
central to	but an afterthought to	collaborative effort
irrelevant to	justifiably embodied by	physical triumph

Step 1—Find the story. In this case, the story is about the public perception of the role of the architect versus the actual role of the architect.

Step 2—Prep your scratch paper. As opposed to columns of A's, B's, C's, D's, E's, and F's, Text Completion scratch paper will look like this:

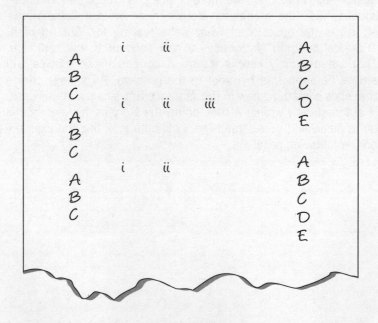

Step 3—Pick a blank. Some blanks will be easier to fill in than others. In general, blanks have two roles. They test either vocabulary or comprehension. A blank testing vocabulary may be easy to fill in with your own words, but then the answer choices may consist of difficult vocabulary words. A blank testing comprehension may depend upon what you put in another blank, or it may contain multiple words, including a few transition words and prepositions. Start with whichever blank seems the easiest. In this case, the last blank may be the easiest.

Step 4—Speak for yourself. The sentence contains the transition word "but." Transition words are always significant. Sensitize yourself to transition words. They always come into play. The passage says that the architect should get lots of credit for a building, BUT...it is clear that other people should get some credit too. Come up with your own words for the blanks. The final product is clearly not "the architects alone."

Step 5—Use POE. There are three choices. "Virtuoso performance" sounds like "the architects alone." Keep it in. "Collaborative effort" is the opposite of what we're looking for. Get rid of it. "Physical triumph" introduces a new concept to the sentence. That automatically knocks it out. A correct answer choice will always be supported by proof in the passage. An answer choice that adds something new to the sentence (physicality, in this case) is automatically wrong. At this point, the story in the sentence is quite clear, and your scratch paper should look like the example on the following page.

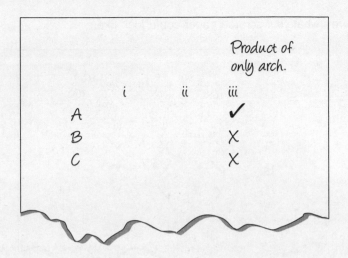

Step 6—Rinse and Repeat. For the first blank, the way buildings are viewed should be similar to the way architects are viewed. Even if you can't come up with a word for the first blank, you at least know that you need something that keeps the sentence going in the same direction. Of the three choices, "at odds with" clearly changes the direction, so get rid of it. "Irrelevant to" is neutral at best, so get rid of it. "Central to" is the only answer choice in the same direction. Give it a check.

For the second blank, thinking in terms of direction will work well again. In this story, what is the relationship between the "artist" and the "architect"? The two seem to serve the same function. You need an answer choice that indicates equivalence. "Justifiably embodied by" is the closest thing in the answer choices to an equals sign.

Here's what your scratch paper could look like:

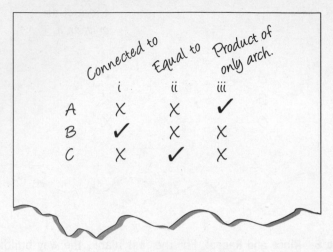

That may seem like a long process, but it's really just a way of thinking. Find the story. Play close attention to transition words. Come up with words for the blank or establish direction. Keep the hand moving and eliminate.

Try one more.

Despite hundreds of (i)_____ attempts to produce a working light bulb, Edison eventually triumphed, his (ii)_____ contributing to his ultimate success.

Blank (i)	Blank (ii)
felicitous	grandiloquence
stymied	indifference
auspicious	tenacity

Who's the main character and what's the story being told? The sentence is about Edison and his attempts to make a working lightbulb. There are two key words in this sentence, "Despite" and "eventually." "Despite" tells you that the sentence has to change direction and "eventually" tells you that it took a long time. The end of the sentence describes his "ultimate success," so the beginning must contain some failure. Put "failed" in for the first blank and eliminate. *Felicitous* (think *felicity*) and *auspicious* are both positive words, so cross them off. *Stymied* stays in. You also know that the process took a long time, so Edison must have been the kind of guy who doesn't give up. Put "stick with it-ness" in for the second blank. You don't have to put a perfect ETS word in the blank. Anything that captures the meaning or idea will do. *Grandiloquence* has to do with the way you talk, which is not what you're looking for, so cross it off. *Indifference* does not mean stubbornness, so get rid of it. You're down to one, so you're done.

Here are a few key concepts to keep in mind.

1. **Scratch Paper**—Using scratch paper favors an efficient "maybe or gone," two-pass approach through the answer choices. With Text Completion questions there are effectively six to nine answer choices rather than five. Scratch paper is crucial.

2. **Clues**—In a regular Sentence Completion question, if the word in the blank is a noun, some other part of the sentence will describe the noun. If it is a verb, there will be some other part of the sentence describing the subject or object of that verb. If it is an adjective, there will invariably be some other part of the sentence describing the noun that the adjective is modifying. This is the essence of what makes a clue a clue. The same concept holds true here but on a slightly larger scale. Whatever information is missing in one sentence must be present in another one. It is the only way for there to be an identifiably correct answer. If the concept of the clue feels too abstract, think of it as

the story being told. Every sentence will tell a story. Who is the main character, what is the main character doing, and what are you told about the main character? If you don't have the story firmly in focus, you're in trouble. The answer choices represent ETS's suggestions for what to put in the blank. In fact, the answer choices have been painstakingly selected and tested with the sole purpose of messing with your head. Unless you can physically put your finger on a clue or key sentence, you are at the mercy of ETS and the answer choices.

3. **Directional Versus Vocabulary**—It is always preferable, or more exact, to come up with your own words for the blank. While sometimes necessary or even effective, simply deciding whether a blank calls for a "good" word or "bad" word can be a crutch for the lazy. With Text Completion questions, however, the answer choices may be all about whether the text will keep the sentence moving in the same direction or the opposite direction. In other words, it is often the transition words or phrases that you are being asked to supply. With only three answer choices, simply identifying either the necessary direction or need for a positive or negative word may take care of all of the elimination you need to get it down to one answer choice.

Know Your Math Vocabulary

Know Your Math Vocabulary

ETS says that the Math section of the GRE tests the "ability to reason quantitatively and to model and solve problems with quantitative methods." Translation: It mostly tests how much you remember from the math courses you took in seventh, eighth, and ninth grades. As you might know, many people study little or no math in college. If the GRE tested "college-level" math, everyone but math majors would bomb. So, junior high math it is. By brushing up on the modest amount of math you need to know for the test, you can significantly increase your GRE Math score.

So, ETS is limited to the math that nearly everyone has studied: arithmetic, basic algebra, basic geometry, and basic statistics. There's no calculus (or even precalculus), no trigonometry, and no advanced algebra or geometry. Because of these limitations, ETS has to resort to tricks and traps in order to create hard problems. Even the most difficult GRE Math problems are typically based on pretty simple principles; what makes some difficult is that the simple principles are disguised with tricky wording. In a way, this is more of a reading test than a math test.

Key Math Terms

Vocabulary in the Math section? Well, if the Math section is just a reading test, then in order to understand what you read, you have to know the language, right?

Quick—what's an integer? Is 0 even or odd? How many even prime numbers are there? These terms look familiar, but it's been a while, right? (We've sorted the terms in alphabetical order, but feel free to skip around.) Review the vocab on the following pages.

- **Consecutive**—Integers listed in order of increasing value without any of the integers in between missing. For example: –3, –2, –1, 0, 1, 2, 3.

- **Decimals**—When you're adding or subtracting decimals, just pretend you're dealing with money. Simply line up the decimal points and proceed as you would if the decimal points weren't there.

$$\begin{array}{r} 34.500 \\ 87.000 \\ 123.456 \\ +\,0.980 \\ \hline 245.936 \end{array}$$

Subtraction works the same way:

$$\begin{array}{r} 17.66 \\ -\;3.2 \\ \hline 14.46 \end{array}$$

To multiply, just proceed as if the decimal points weren't there. Then put in the decimal point afterward, counting the total number of digits to the right of the decimal points in the numbers you are multiplying. Then, place the decimal point in your solution so that you have the same number of digits to the right of it:

$$\begin{array}{r} 3.451 \\ \times\;\;\;8.9 \\ \hline 30.7139 \end{array}$$

There are a total of 4 digits to the right of the two numbers being multiplied above, so there are four decimal places in the solution. Except for placing the decimal point, this is exactly what you would have done if multiplying 3,451 and 89.

To divide, set up the problem as a fraction, then move the decimal point in the divisor (aka the number you are dividing by) all the way to the right. Then move the decimal point in the number being divided the same number of places to the right. For example:

$$\frac{24}{1.25} = \frac{2400}{125} = 19.2$$

Remember that the GRE has an on-screen calculator. You can work through most problems involving decimals simply by using the calculator.

- **Difference**—The result of subtraction.

- **Digit**—The numbers 0, 1, 2, 3, 4, 5, 6, 7, 8, and 9. Just think of them as the numbers on your phone. The number 189.75 has five digits: 1, 8, 9, 7, and 5. Five is the hundredths digit, 7 is the tenths digit, 9 is the units digit, 8 is the tens digit, and 1 is the hundreds digit.

- **Distinct**—Different. For example, the integer 123 has 3 distinct digits, while the integer 122 has 2 distinct digits.

- **Divisible**—When one integer is divisible by another, the result is also an integer. For example, 6 is divisible by 3 because the result is 2, an integer. An integer is divisible by 2 if its units digit is divisible by 2. An integer is divisible by 3 if the sum of its digits is divisible by 3. (For example, 123 is divisible by 3 because $1 + 2 + 3 = 6$ and 6 is divisible by 3.) An integer is divisible by 5 if its units digit is either 0 or 5. An integer is divisible by 10 if its units digit is 0.

- **Even/Odd**—An even number is any integer that can be divided evenly by 2 (like 4, 8, and 22); any integer is even if its units digit is even. An odd number is any integer that can't be divided evenly by 2 (like 3, 7, and 31); any integer is odd if its units digit is odd. Put another way, even integers have a remainder of 0 when divided by 2 while odd integers have a remainder of 1 when divided by 2.

  Here are some rules that apply to even and odd integers: Even + even = even; odd + odd = even; even + odd = odd; even × even = even; odd × odd = odd; even × odd = even. What if you aren't sure about the rule? Just try some numbers. For example, even + even is even because 2 + 4 = 6, which is even. Don't confuse *odd* and *even* with *positive* and *negative*. The terms *even* and *odd* apply only to integers, so fractions are neither even nor odd.

- **Exponent**—Exponents are a sort of mathematical shorthand. Instead of writing (2)(2)(2)(2), write 2^4. The little 4 is called an "exponent" and the big 2 is called a "base."

  There are primary exponent rules. We call these the MADSPM rules. MADSPM stands for Multiply-Add, Divide-Subtract, and Power-Multiply. Here's how it works.

  To multiply exponent expressions that have the same base, add the exponents. For example, $2^2 \times 2^4 = 2^{2+4} = 2^6$ and $(x^3)(x^4) = x^{3+4} = x^7$.

  To divide exponent expressions that have the same base, subtract the exponents. For example, $2^6 \div 2^4 = 2^{6-4} = 2^2$ and $\frac{x^7}{x^4} = x^{7-4} = x^3$.

  When an exponent expression is raised to a power, multiply the exponents. For example, $(2^2)^3 = 2^{2 \times 3} = 2^6$ and $(x^3)^4 = x^{3 \times 4} = x^{12}$.

If you are ever unsure of one of these rules, just remember: When in doubt, expand it out. For example, $2^2 \times 2^4 = (2)(2) \times (2)(2)(2)(2) = 2^6$.

Here Are Some Additional Exponent Rules

Raising a number greater than 1 to a power greater than 1 results in a bigger number. For example, $2^2 = 4$.

Raising a fraction between 0 and 1 to a power greater than 1 results in a smaller number. For example, $\left(\frac{1}{2}\right)^2 = \frac{1}{4}$.

A negative number raised to an even power results in a positive number. For example, $(-2)^2 = 4$.

A negative number raised to an odd power results in a negative number. For example, $(-2)^3 = -8$.

When you see a number raised to an negative exponent, just put a 1 over it and get rid of the negative sign. For example, $(2)^{-2} = \left(\frac{1}{2}\right)^2$, which $= \frac{1}{4}$.

- **Factor**—Integer a is a factor of integer b if the result when b is divided by a is an integer. For example, 1, 2, 3, 4, 6, and 12 are all factors of 12 because the result when 12 is divided by any of these integers is also an integer. All numbers, even prime numbers, have at least two factors: one and the number itself. To find factors, it's best to list the factors in pairs. For example, the factors of 24 are 1 and 24, 2 and 12, 3 and 8, and 4 and 6. You know you've found all the factors when there are no integers between the last pair of factors that also divide evenly into your starting number.

- **Fractions**—A fraction is just shorthand for division. On the GRE, you'll probably be asked to compare, add, subtract, multiply, and divide fractions. To multiply fractions, just multiply the numerators (the tops of the fractions) and denominators (the bottoms of the fractions) straight across.

$$\frac{4}{5} \times \frac{2}{3} = \frac{8}{15}$$

To divide, you multiply by the second fraction's reciprocal; in other words, turn the second fraction upside down. Put its denominator over its numerator, then multiply:

$$\frac{4}{5} \div \frac{2}{3} = \frac{4}{5} \times \frac{3}{2} = \frac{12}{10} = \frac{6}{5}$$

If you were asked to compare $\frac{3}{7}$ and $\frac{7}{14}$, all you have to do is multiply diagonally up from each denominator, as shown:

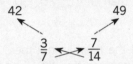

Now, just compare 42 to 49. Because 49 is greater, that means $\frac{7}{14}$ is the greater fraction. This technique is called the *Bowtie*. You can also use the Bowtie to add or subtract fractions with different denominators. Just multiply the denominators of the two fractions, and then multiply diagonally up from each denominator, as shown:

$$\frac{3}{4} + \frac{2}{7} = \frac{{}^{21}3}{4} \quad \times \quad \frac{2{}^{8}}{7} = \frac{21}{28} + \frac{8}{28} = \frac{29}{28}$$

$$\frac{3}{4} - \frac{2}{7} = \frac{{}^{21}3}{4} \quad \times \quad \frac{2{}^{8}}{7} = \frac{21}{28} - \frac{8}{28} = \frac{13}{28}$$

If the denominators are the same, you don't need the Bowtie. You just keep the same denominator and add or subtract the numerators, as shown below.

$$\frac{1}{9} + \frac{2}{9} + \frac{4}{9} = \frac{1+2+4}{9} = \frac{7}{9}$$

$$\frac{7}{9} - \frac{4}{9} - \frac{2}{9} = \frac{7-4-2}{9} = \frac{1}{9}$$

- **Integer**—Integers are whole numbers. Integers can be positive or negative. Zero is also an integer. All of the following are integers: –5, –4, –3, –2, –1, 0, 1, 2, 3, 4, 5, 6. Note that fractions, such as $\frac{1}{2}$, are *not* integers. Neither are decimals.

- **Multiple**—A multiple of a number is that number multiplied by an integer other than 0. 10, 20, 30, 40, 50, and 60 are all multiples of 10.

- **Nonnegative**—All the positive numbers plus zero. If ETS uses this term rather than *positive*, it will be important to remember to think about zero.

- **Order of operations**—Also known as PEMDAS, or Please Excuse My Dear Aunt Sally. Parentheses > Exponents > Multiplication = Division > Addition = Subtraction. This is the order in which the operations are to be performed. For example:

$$10 - (6 - 5) - (3 + 3) - 3 =$$

Start with the operations inside the parentheses. The operation inside the first pair of parentheses, 6 − 5, equals 1. The operation inside the second pair equals 6. Now rewrite the problem, as shown below.

$$10 - 1 - 6 - 3 =$$

$$9 - 6 - 3 =$$

$$3 - 3 =$$

$$= 0$$

Here's another example:

Say you were asked to compare $(3 \times 2)^2$ and $(3)(2^2)$. $(3 \times 2)^2 = 6^2$, or 36, and $(3)(2^2) = 3 \times 4$, or 12.

Note that with multiplication and division, you just go left to right (hence the "=" sign in the description of PEMDAS above). Same with addition and subtraction. In other words, if the only operations you have to perform are multiplication and division, you don't have to do all multiplication first, because multiplication and division are equivalent operations. Just go left to right.

- **Positive/Negative**—Positive numbers increase as they move away from zero (6 is greater than 5); negative numbers decrease as they move away from zero (−6 is less than −5). Note that zero is the only number that is neither positive nor negative. Positive × positive = positive; negative × negative = positive; positive × negative = negative. Be careful not to confuse positive and negative with odd and even.

- **Prime**—A prime number is a number that is evenly divisible only by itself and by 1. Zero and 1 are not prime numbers, and 2 is the only even prime number. Other prime numbers include 3, 5, 7, 11, and 13 (but there are many more).

- **Prime factors**—Prime factors are factors of a number that are also prime. For example, the prime factors of 12 are 3 and 2. To find prime factors, use a factor tree.

- **Probability**—Probability is equal to the outcome you're looking for divided by the total outcomes. If it is impossible for something to happen, the probability of it happening is equal to 0. If something is certain to happen, the probability is equal to 1. If it is possible for something to happen, but not necessary, the probability is between 0 and 1. For example, if you flip a coin, what's the probability that it will land on "heads"? One out of two, or $\frac{1}{2}$. What is the probability that it won't land on "heads"? One out of two, or $\frac{1}{2}$.

- **Product**—The result of multiplication.

- **Quotient**—The result of division.

- **Reducing fractions**—To reduce a fraction, "cancel" or cross out factors that are common to both the numerator and the denominator. For example, to reduce $\frac{18}{24}$, just divide both 18 and 24 by the greatest common factor, 6. That leaves you with $\frac{3}{4}$. If you couldn't think of 6, both 18 and 24 are even, so just start cutting each in half (or in thirds) until you can't go any further. And remember—you cannot reduce numbers across an equals sign (=), a plus sign (+), or a minus sign (–).

- **Remainder**—The remainder is the number left over when one integer cannot be divided evenly by another. The remainder is always an integer. Remember grade school math class? It's the number that came after the big "R." For example, the remainder when 7 is divided by 4 is 3 because 4 goes into 7 one time with 3 left over. ETS likes remainder questions because you can't do them on your calculator.

- **Square root**—The sign $\sqrt{}$ indicates the square root of a number. For example, $\sqrt{2}$ means to find the number that multiplied by itself equals 2. You can't add or subtract square roots unless they have the same number under the root sign ($\sqrt{2} + \sqrt{3}$ does not equal $\sqrt{5}$, but $\sqrt{2} + \sqrt{2} = 2\sqrt{2}$). You can multiply and divide them just like regular integers:

$$\sqrt{2} \times \sqrt{3} = \sqrt{6}$$

$$\sqrt{6} \div \sqrt{3} = \sqrt{2}$$

You will have a square root symbol on your calculator, but it is often easier if you know the values of some commonly used roots. Here are a few square roots to remember that might come in handy:

$$\sqrt{1} = 1$$

$$\sqrt{2} = 1.4$$

$$\sqrt{3} = 1.7$$

$$\sqrt{4} = 2$$

Note: If you're told that $X^2 = 16$, then $X = \pm 4$. You must be especially careful to remember this on Quantitative Comparison questions. But if you're asked for the value $\sqrt{16}$, you are being asked for the positive root only, so the answer is 4. A square root is always nonnegative.

- **Standard deviation**—The standard deviation of a group of data points is a measure of the group's variation from its mean. You'll rarely, if ever, have to actually calculate the standard deviation, so just remember this: The greater the standard deviation, the more widely dispersed the values are. The smaller the standard deviation, the more closely grouped the values are around the mean. For example, the standard deviation of the numbers 6, 0, and 6 is greater than the standard deviation of the numbers 4, 4, and 4, because 6, 0, and 6 are more widely dispersed than 4, 4, and 4.

- **Sum**—The result of addition.

- **Zero**—An integer that's neither positive nor negative but is even. The sum of 0 and any other number is that other number; the product of 0 and any other number is 0.

Quantitative Comparison

There are four question formats on the Math section: five-choice Problem-Solving questions, four-choice Quantitative Comparisons (or quant comps), All that Apply consisting of three to eight answer choices, and Numeric Entry in which you have to type your own answer into a box. A Quant Comp is a math question that consists of two quantities, one in Quantity A and one in Quantity B. You compare the two quantities and choose:

(A) Quantity A is greater.

(B) Quantity B is greater.

(C) The quantities are equal.

(D) The relationship cannot be determined from the information given.

Quant Comps have only four answer choices. That's great: A blind guess has one chance in four of being correct. So, the odds of guessing correctly on a Quant Comp start off better than the odds for guessing correctly on a Problem-Solving question. Always write A, B, C, D (but no E) on your scratch paper so that you can cross off wrong answer choices as you go. The content of Quant Comp problems is drawn from the same basic arithmetic, algebra, and geometry concepts that are used on GRE Math problems in other formats. In general, then, you'll apply the same techniques that you use on other types of math questions. Still, Quant Comps do require a few special techniques of their own.

The Peculiar Behavior of Choice (D)

There are only two options when two numbers are compared. Either one number is greater than the other or the two numbers are equal. So, when both quantities in a Quant Comp problem contain numbers, it's always possible to determine the relationship. Therefore, the fourth bubble, or (D), can be eliminated immediately on all such problems. For example:

Quantity A	Quantity B
$\dfrac{2}{3}$	$\dfrac{3}{4}$

○ Quantity A is greater.

○ Quantity B is greater.

○ The two quantities are equal.

○ The relationship cannot be determined from the information given.

You know the answer can be determined, so the answer could never be (D). So right off the bat, as soon as you see a Quant Comp that involves only numbers, you can eliminate (D) on your scratch paper. The answer to this one is (B), by the way. Use the Bowtie so you end up with 8 versus 9.

Compare Before You Calculate

You don't always have to figure out the exact values for both columns to make the comparison. The prime directive is to compare the two columns. Finding ETS's answer frequently is merely a matter of simplifying, reducing, factoring, or expanding. For example:

Quantity A	Quantity B
$\frac{1}{17} + \frac{1}{8} + \frac{1}{5}$	$\frac{1}{5} + \frac{1}{17} + \frac{1}{7}$

○ Quantity A is greater.

○ Quantity B is greater.

○ The two quantities are equal.

○ The relationship cannot be determined from the information given.

First, eliminate (D), because there are only numbers in both columns. Then, notice that there are fractions common to both columns; both contain $\frac{1}{17}$ and $\frac{1}{5}$. If the same numbers are in both columns, they can't make a difference to the total value. So just cross them off (after copying down the problem on your scratch paper, of course). Now, what's left? Quantity A is $\frac{1}{8}$, and Quantity B is $\frac{1}{7}$. All you have to do now is compare $\frac{1}{8}$ to $\frac{1}{7}$. Use the Bowtie to get (B).

Turning Algebra into Arithmetic

The Problem with GRE Algebra

Imagine going to a candy story to purchase 10 pieces of candy for 5 cents each. How much change would you get if you gave the clerk a one-dollar bill?

The answer is obviously 50 cents. Even if the numbers were a little more difficult, the arithmetic to solve the problem is pretty simple. For instance, if you purchase 8 pieces of candy for 30 cents each and you give the clerk a five-dollar bill, how much change would you receieve? The process to find the answer is exactly the same as before. You would still multiply 8 pieces of candy by 30 cents and subtract that product from five dollars to get $2.60. Since we use operations like this on a daily basis, it's common to think in terms of actual numbers because arithmetic is more comfortable.

However, GRE questions often do not use actual numbers. Instead, test takers are offered variables and the simple questions described above are written more like:

> If Sydney goes to a candy store to purchase p pieces of candy for c cents each and pays the clerk d dollars, then what is her change?

A common approach to this algebra question would be to multiply p and c and then subtract that product from d, as we did in the earlier problems. This would give us $d - pc$, which would be wrong because it does not account for converting the cents into dollars. Try it out using the numbers from the first example if you don't believe us. Replace p with 10, c with 5, and d with 1. The resulting expression is $1 - (10)(5)$, which equals -49.

However, you can be sure that the GRE would have $d - pc$ as a possible answer choice that many test takers would choose, never realizing it is not the correct answer. Because we rarely do algebra, we're more prone to make mistakes that are easily avoid-able when using arithmetic.

Considering we're better at arithmetic than we are at algebra, it is in our best interest to turn algebra problems into arithmetic! To do this, simply Plug In real numbers for the variables in algebra problems. Performing addition, subtraction, multiplication, and division operations, as we did in the versions of the candy store problem that used real numbers, was far simpler than thinking in terms of variables. Anytime you see an algebra question on the GRE, be ready to use actual numbers rather than variables. Here's an example:

> Kyle has four fewer toys than Scott but seven more toys than Jody. If Kyle has k toys, then how many toys do Scott and Jody have together?
>
> ○ $2k + 11$
>
> ○ $2k + 7$
>
> ○ $2k + 3$
>
> ○ $2k - 3$
>
> ○ $2k - 11$

Step 1—Recognize the opportunity. When variables appear in the answer choices, be ready to Plug In.

Step 2—Set up your scratch paper. Write A, B, C, D, and E in a column on your scratch paper.

Step 3—Plug In an easy number. Since it's easier to think of ten toys than it is to think of k toys, Plug In a number for the value k. Be sure to choose a number that will make the math easy, such as 2, 5, 10, or 100. Let's say $k = 10$. Write this down on the scratch paper.

Step 4—Work the problem. Now work the problem. Kyle has four fewer toys than Scott has. If Kyle has 10, then Scott has 14. Write down $s = 14$ on the scratch paper. Kyle has 7 more toys than Jodi has. Therefore, Jodi has three toys. Write $j = 3$ on the scratch paper.

Step 5—Circle the target number. The target number is the number that the question ultimately asks for. In this case, the question asks, "How many toys do Scott and Jody have together?" Since Scott has 14 and Jodi has 3, the target number is 17. Write it down and circle it.

Step 6—Check all the answer choices. Anywhere there is a k in the answer choices, Plug In 10. Remember to look for an answer choice to equal 17, the target number.

(A) $2(10) + 11 = 31$. Nope. Cross it off.

(B) $2(10) + 7 = 27$. Nope. Cross it off.

(C) $2(10) + 3 = 23$. Nope. Cross it off.

(D) $2(10) - 3 = 17$. This looks good, but always check all answer choices.

(E) $2(10) - 11 = 9$. Nope.

The answer is (D). Here's what your scratch paper could look like:

A̶ 20 + 11   K = 10
B̶ 20 + 7   S = 14   ⑰
C̶ 20 + 3   J = 3
✓(D 20 − 3)
E̶ 20 − 11

Here are a couple of things to keep in mind about Plugging In:

- **Do all work on the scratch paper.** When you're done, you should see all variables given numeric values, a target number circled, and all answer choices checked.

- **Keep the math easy.** If you Plug In a number and the math gets complicated, don't panic; just change the number that you Plugged In.

- **Check to see if more than one answer choice works.** If so, Plug In a new number, find a new target number, and only check the answer choices that remain. Continue this process until there is only one answer choice left.

- **Know what not to Plug In.** Avoid Plugging In 0, 1, the same number for multiple variables, or numbers that you find in the question. These numbers are not necessarily going to give you the wrong answer, but they are more likely to yield two answer choices that match the target number. This will then force you to do more work by Plugging In again.

Plugging In on Quantitative Comparisons

You will also see Quantitative Comparison questions with unknown quantities. Use these opportunities to Plug In, as well.

$$y \neq 0$$

Quantity A	**Quantity B**
$-10y$	$-y$

○ Quantity A is greater.

○ Quantity B is greater.

○ The two quantities are equal.

○ The relationship cannot be determined from the information given.

Step 1—Recognize the opportunity. The first thing to notice is that it is a Quantitative Comparison problem. The second thing to notice is unknown quantities. This indicates that it is a Quant Comp Plug In question.

Step 2—Set up your scratch paper. Write A, B, C, and D horizontally on the scratch paper, with columns for Quantity A and Quantity B on either side, as shown on the scratch paper on the following page.

Step 3—Plug In an easy number. Make $y = 2$. This would transform the value of Quantity A from $-10y$ into -20 and the value of Quantity B from $-y$ into -2. Write these down in the Quantity A and Quantity B columns on the scratch paper.

Step 4—Eliminate two of answers A, B, and C. Determine that the greater value is -2, which is Quantity B. Clearly Quantity A is not *always* going to be greater, nor will the answers *always* be equal. Therefore, eliminate (A) and (C). This step will always lead to the elimination of two answer choices. Now determine whether (B) is always the greater value.

Step 5—Repeat using FROZEN. After Plugging In an easy number, test out whether (B) will always be correct by using trickier numbers. To know which tricky numbers to use, think of the acronym FROZEN. It stands for all the weird numbers that you might normally shy away from, or not think of, when Plugging In the first time: *Fractions, Repeats from the problem, One, Zero, Extreme numbers,* and *Negatives.* Determine which of these types of numbers might yield a value of Quantity B that is less than that of Quantity A. Since the problem asks about negative numbers, that is a good place to start. Make $y = -2$. Quantity A is now 20, while Quantity B is 2. Quantity A is greater, so eliminate (B). The correct answer is (D).

Here is what your scratch paper could look like:

```
   A      A̶ B̶ C̶ (D)    B
  -20       y = 2       -2
   20       y = -2       2
            y =
```

Be sure to keep Plugging In until you have eliminated (A), (B), and (C) or you have tried enough types of FROZEN numbers to reasonably conclude an answer. If after going through a number of FROZEN numbers, and (A), (B), or (C) remains, it is likely the correct answer.

Try one more:

$$0 < x < 10$$
$$0 < y < 1$$

Quantity A	**Quantity B**
$x - y$	9

○ Quantity A is greater.

○ Quantity B is greater.

○ The two quantities are equal.

○ The relationship cannot be determined from the information given.

Step 1—Recognize the opportunity. There are unknown quantities (x and y), so this is an opportunity to Plug In.

Step 2—Set up your scratch paper. Write A, B, C, and D horizontally on the scratch paper, with columns for Quantity A and Quantity B on either side.

Step 3—Plug In an easy number. On this problem, there are ranges for x and y, so Plug In the greatest x and the least y to find the maximum range for $x - y$. Make $x = 9$ and $y = 0.1$. Quantity A now equals 8.9 and Quantity B equals 9.

Step 4—Eliminate two of answers A, B, and C. Since Quantity B is the greater value, eliminate (A) and (C).

Step 5—Repeat using FROZEN. Consult the FROZEN numbers to find a way to eliminate (B). A fraction and a repeated number from the problem (in this case, 9) have been used. Zero and negative numbers are not eligible according to the constraints of the problem. Try extreme numbers. The value of x has to be less than 10, so 9.9 is about as extreme as x can be. Make $x = 9.9$ and $y = 0.1$, and $x - y$ will now equal 9.8, which is greater than 9. Eliminate (B) and choose (D).

Must Be

There are other questions besides Quantitative Comparisons that may require you to Plug In more than once before you find the correct answer. Take a look at this question.

> The positive difference between
> the squares of any two consecutive
> integers, x and $x + 1$, must be
>
> ○ the square of an integer
> ○ a multiple of 5
> ○ an even integer
> ○ an odd number
> ○ a prime number

The phrase "must be" is a clue to let you know that not only are you going to have to Plug In, but you will also likely have to do it more than once. In that respect, you can treat these the same way you do Quantitative Comparisons.

Step 1—Recognize the opportunity. The phrase "must be" in a question is a trigger that indicates a Plug In question.

Step 2—Set up your scratch paper. After seeing "must be," mark down A, B, C, D, and E in a vertical column. To the right of your column, leave spaces for the variables. It could look like this:

$$x = \qquad x = \qquad x =$$
$$y = \qquad y = \qquad y =$$

A
B
C
D
E

Step 3—Plug In an easy number. Try $x = 2$. If $x = 2$, then $x + 1 = 3$.

Step 4—Eliminate incorrect answer choices. The squares are 4 and 9, and the positive difference is 5. Choice (A) does not work, so eliminate it. Choice (B) works, so keep it. Eliminate (C) since it does not work. Choices (D) and (E) both work, so keep them.

Step 5—Repeat using FROZEN. Since "must be" is a clue to Plug In more than once, Plug In again using FROZEN numbers to try and eliminate more answer choices. Try an extreme number, such as $x = 10$. When Plugging In 10, the squares are 100 and 121. The difference is 21. Choice (B) no longer works, so eliminate it. Keep (D) since it still works. And eliminate (E), which does not work. The only answer choice remaining is (D), which is the correct answer. Your scratch paper could look like this:

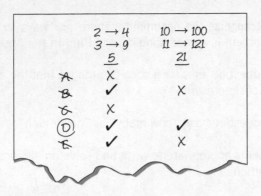

$2 \rightarrow 4$ $10 \rightarrow 100$
$3 \rightarrow 9$ $11 \rightarrow 121$
$\underline{5}$ $\underline{21}$

A X
B ✓ X
C X
(D) ✓ ✓
E ✓ X

PITA

There is one more kind of Plugging In strategy. It is called PITA, which stands for Plugging In the Answers. It is one of the most powerful types of Plugging In because it can take some of the hardest problems on the GRE and turn them into simple arithmetic. The hardest thing about this technique, however, is remembering when to use it. Take a look at this question:

> Two positive integers, x and y, have a
>
> difference of 15. If the smaller integer, y,
>
> is $\frac{5}{8}$ of x, then what is the value of y ?
>
> ◯ 40
> ◯ 25
> ◯ 20
> ◯ 15
> ◯ 10

Step 1—Recognize the opportunity. There are ways to know if a certain problem is a good candidate to Plug In the Answers:

- the question asks for a specific amount that the answer choices represent

- the questions ask "how many" or "how much"

- it seems appropriate to write and solve an algebraic equation

Step 2—List the answer choices on your scratch paper. Write down the answer choices (in this case 40, 25, 20, 15, and 10) in a vertical column.

Step 3—Label the answer choices. The question asks, "What is the value of y?" The answer choices, therefore, represent potential values for y. Label the first column (the one with the answer choices) "y."

Step 4—Plug In (C). Since the answer choices are listed in ascending or descending order, it will be helpful to start with (C). Assume for a moment that the middle value is the correct answer choice. If $y = 20$, then what else would be true?

Step 5—Work the problem in bite-sized pieces, making a new column for each new step. The problem says that y is $\frac{5}{8}$ of x. So if $y = 20$, then $x = 32$. Make a column labeled "x" and write 32 in the column next to the 20.

Step 6—POE. What would have to happen for (C) to be the correct answer? There must be a difference of 15 between x and y. With (C), there is a difference of 12. Cross off (C). Because the difference needs to be greater, the numbers need to be greater. Therefore, also eliminate (D) and (E), as those choices are less than (C). This is why it is useful to start PITA problems with (C). Because the answer choices are listed in either ascending or descending numerical order, if it's possible to determine the value of (C) is either greater or less than needed, it's also possible to eliminate the answer choices that are greater or less than (C). At this point, only two answer choices remain. Treat the columns like a spreadsheet for the remaining answers. Fill in the rest of the row for (B) where $y = 25$. Moving right, it is evident that $x = 40$. The difference is 15, which is exactly what the question is looking for. With PITA questions, only one answer choice can work, so there is no need to check out every answer choice. Choice (B) is correct. Here is what your scratch paper could look like:

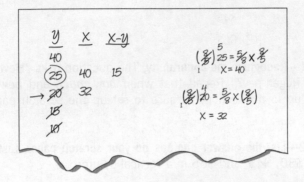

Try one more.

> Vicken, Roger, and Adam buy a $90 radio. If Roger agrees to pay twice as much as Adam and Vicken agrees to pay three times as much as Roger, how much must Roger pay?
>
> ○ $10
> ○ $20
> ○ $30
> ○ $45
> ○ $65

Step 1—Recognize the opportunity. The question asks "How much must Roger pay?" Recall that when *how much* and *how many* show up in a question, be sure to set up the scratch paper for PITA.

Step 2—List the answer choices on your scratch paper. List $10, $20, $30, $45, and $65 in a vertical column.

Step 3—Label the answer choices. What do those numbers represent? The amount Roger pays. Label this first column Roger (or "R" for short).

Step 4—Plug In (C). Assume Roger pays $30.

Step 5—Work the problem in bite-sized pieces, making a new column for each new step. If Roger pays $30, then Adam pays $15. Make a column for Adam with $15 written under that column in the same row as (C). Vicken pays $90, so likewise make a column for Vicken with $90 written under it.

Step 6—POE. Add up all the three men's contributions to find a total of $135, which is greater than what the problem states the radio actually costs. Eliminate (C). Since (C) is too great, also eliminate (D) and (E), which are even greater. Fill in the columns for (B). If Roger pays $20, then Adam pays $10 and Vicken pays $60. All three combine to pay $90, which is what the problem states they actually paid. The correct answer is (B).

Your scratch paper could look like this:

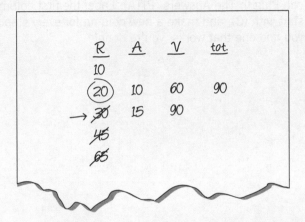

To review, there are four kinds of Plugging In:

1. **Plugging In for Variables.** When you see variables in the answer choices, Plug In. Make sure you give the variables numeric values, circle the target number, and check all answer choices.

2. **Quantitative Comparison Plug In.** When you see unknown values on Quantitative Comparison questions, set up for Plugging In. Use an easier number first and then go through the FROZEN numbers until you are left with one answer choice.

3. Must Be. "Must be" means that you should be ready to Plug In more than once. Put answer choices in a vertical column and leave space above to Plug In for a variety of variables. Remember to start with an easy number and then go through the FROZEN numbers until you are left with one answer choice.

4. PITA. When a question asks "how much," "how many," or for a specific value that the answer choices represent, you can Plug In The Answers (PITA). Label the first column, start with (C), and make a new column for every step. When you find one that works, you're done!

Find the Missing Pieces in Geometry

Find the Missing Pieces in Geometry

Geometry on the GRE is really like a series of brainteasers. It is your job to find the missing piece of information. They will always give you four out of five pieces of information, and you will always be able to find the fifth. There are only about one-half dozen concepts that show up. Once you learn to recognize them, you should be able to handle any problems you might see. The basic problems are made up of parallel lines, triangles, circles, and quadrilaterals.

First, a few basics:

Line—A line (which can be thought of as a perfectly flat angle) is a 180-degree angle.

Perpendicular—When two lines are perpendicular to each other, their intersection forms four 90-degree angles.

Right angle—90-degree angles are also called right angles. A right angle is identified by a little box at the intersection of the angle's sides:

Vertical angles—Vertical angles are the angles across from each other that are formed by the intersection of two lines. The degree measures of vertical angles are equal.

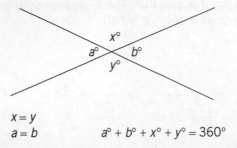

$x = y$
$a = b$ $a° + b° + x° + y° = 360°$

Parallel lines—First, never assume two lines are parallel unless that is stated in the problem or you can prove it from the information in the problem. When you see the symbol for parallel lines, however, there's generally only one thing interesting about parallel lines. When you see a pair of parallel lines intersected by a third line, two kinds of angles are formed: big ones and small ones. All big angles are equal to all big angles and all small angles are equal to all small angles. Any big + any small = 180°. When you see the symbol for parallel lines, always and automatically identify the big angles and the small angles. They are almost assuredly going to come into play. Otherwise, why make them parallel?

For example, take a look at the following figure. The angle marked 40° is a small angle. (The small angles are the angles with degree measures less than or equal to 90°.) The angle marked *a* is also a small angle, so it is also 40°. The angle marked *b* is a large angle. Since big + small = 180°, *b* is 140°.

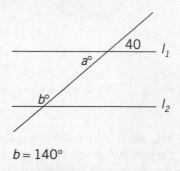

$b = 140°$

Triangles

There are several basic facts that ETS expects you to know about triangles. The degree measures of the three angles add up to 180°. The longest side is opposite the largest angle, just as the shortest side is opposite the smallest angle. The formula for the area of a triangle is $A = \frac{1}{2}(b)(h)$. An equilateral triangle is one in which the lengths of all three sides are equal. Also, the three angles have equal measures and are all 60°. An isosceles triangle is one in which two of the sides are equal in length. Naturally, sides opposite equal angles are equal in length and vice versa.

A lesser-known triangle rule is the *Third Side Rule*. The length of the third side of a triangle is always less than the sum of the lengths of the other two sides, but greater than their difference.

The most frequently tested triangles on the GRE are right triangles. A right triangle has one 90° angle and two smaller angles. If you know the lengths of two sides of a right triangle, you can always find the length of the third using the Pythagorean Theorem. The Pythagorean Theorem states that $a^2 + b^2 = c^2$ where c is the hypotenuse. The hypotenuse of a right triangle is the longest side of the triangle. The hypotenuse is also the side opposite the right angle.

It's good to understand how the Pythagorean Theorem works, but you rarely need to use it because there are three right triangles that come up all the time. Once you recognize these three right triangles, you can save yourself some time because you won't need to do the calculations. So be on the lookout for right triangles on the GRE! If you see a triangle and it is a right triangle, be extremely suspicious. It is likely to be one of three common right triangles. The common right triangles are Pythagorean triples, 45-45-90 triangles, and 30-60-90 triangles.

Pythagorean Triples

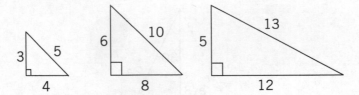

The Pythagorean Theorem is true for any right triangle, but when all three sides are integers, it's called a Pythagorean triple. Note the second triple in the diagram above: 6-8-10. See how it's a multiple of the 3-4-5 triple? Any multiple of a Pythagorean triple is also a Pythagorean triple. If you see a right triangle, start looking for Pythagorean triples. As long as two of the sides match one of the triangles above, you do not need to calculate the third side.

45-45-90

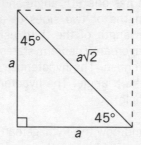

When a square (all sides are equal, all angles are 90°) is cut in half along one of its diagonals, the result is two 45-45-90 triangles. If each side of the square is a, then the diagonal of the square (also known as the hypotenuse of the right triangle) is $a\sqrt{2}$. If a problem has a right triangle and a $\sqrt{2}$ in it, think 45-45-90 triangle. One common use for the 45-45-90 triangle on the GRE is to find the length of the diagonal of a square for which you know either the length of the side or the area.

30-60-90

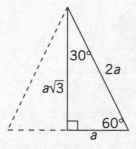

When an equilateral triangle is cut in half, the result is two 30-60-90 triangles. One angle is still 60°. The angle at the top got cut in half and is now 30°. The angle at the base is 90°. If the small side of the new triangle is a, then the big side (opposite the 90° angle) is $2a$. The middle side, opposite the 60° angle, is $a\sqrt{3}$. One common use for the 30-60-90 triangle on the GRE is to find the area of an equilateral triangle. If you know the length of the side of the equilateral triangle, you can use the 30-60-90 relationship to find the equilateral triangle's height. If a problem has a right triangle and a $\sqrt{3}$, look for a 30-60-90 triangle.

Circles

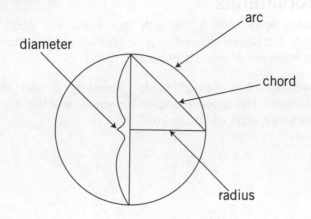

Circle Facts

- All circles contain 360°.

- The radius of a circle is the line that connects the center of the circle to a point on the circumference of the circle.

- The diameter is a line that connects two points on the circumference of the circle and goes through the center of the circle. The diameter is the longest line that can be drawn in a circle. The length of the diameter is twice that of the radius.

- The formula for the area of a circle is $A = \pi r^2$.

- The formula for the circumference (perimeter) of a circle is $C = \pi d$, or $C = 2\pi r$.

If you know the radius, you can find anything else you need to know about a circle. You should be comfortable going from circumference to radius to area and back. Remember that pi equals approximately 3.14, but as a general rule, leave it as pi.

Quadrilaterals

Four-sided figure—Any figure with four sides has 360°. That includes rectangles, squares, and parallelograms (four-sided figures made out of two sets of parallel lines).

Parallelogram—A four-sided figure consisting of two sets of parallel lines. The opposite angles are equal, and the big angle and the small angle add up to 180°.

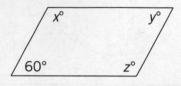

$x = 120°$, $y = 60°$, $z = 120°$

Rectangle—A four-sided figure where opposite sides are parallel and all angles are 90°. The area of a rectangle is length times width ($A = lw$).

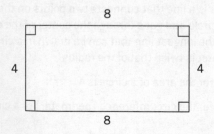

perimeter = 4 + 8 + 4 + 8 = 24
area = 8 × 4 = 32

Square—A square is a rectangle with four equal sides. The area is the length of any side times itself, which is to say, the length of any side squared ($A = s^2$).

A Few Other Odds and Ends

Coordinate geometry—This involves a grid where the horizontal line is the x-axis and the vertical line is the y-axis. In an ordered pair, the x-coordinate always comes first, and the y-coordinate always comes second.

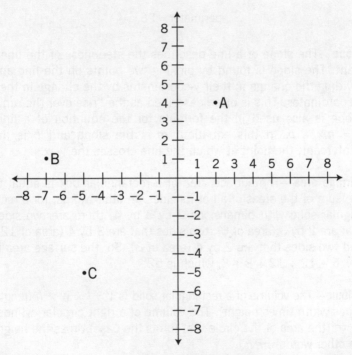

The ordered pair for point A on the diagram above is (2, 4) because the x-coordinate is 2 over from the origin (0, 0) and the y-coordinate is 4 above the origin. Point B is at (–7, 1). Point C is at (–5, –5).

Inscribed—One figure is inscribed within another when points on the edge of the enclosed figure touch the outer figure.

Perimeter—The perimeter of a rectangle, square, parallelogram, triangle, or any sided figure is the sum of the lengths of the sides:

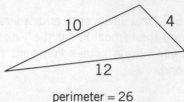

perimeter = 26

Slope—The slope of a line describes the steepness of the line's slant. The slope is found by picking two points on the line and dividing the change in their *y*-coordinates by the change in their *x*-coordinates. This is often described as the "rise over the run." Slope is also used in the formula for the equation of a line: $y = mx + b$. In this equation, m is the slope and b is the *y*-intercept, the point at which the line crosses the *y*-axis.

Surface area—The surface area of a rectangular box is equal to the sum of the areas of all of its sides. In other words, for a rectangular solid with dimensions 2 by 3 by 4, there are two sides that are 2 by 3 (area of 6), two sides that are 3 by 4 (area of 12), and two sides that are 2 by 4 (area of 8). So, the surface area is 6 + 6 + 12 + 12 + 8 + 8, which is 52.

Volume—The volume of a rectangular solid is $V = l \times w \times h$ (length times width times height). The volume of a right circular cylinder is πr^2 (the area of the circle that forms the base) times the height (in other words, $\pi r^2 h$).

The Basic Approach

Step 1—Draw the figure. You will need to work with the figures and fill in lots of pieces of information, so it is important to draw the figure on your scratch paper. Try to draw the figure to scale, but remember to base your drawing upon what you're told, not necessarily what you're shown on screen. Drawing your own figure is particularly important when the problem doesn't provide you with one.

Step 2—Fill in what you know. The problem will give you various pieces of information. It might give you an angle or two, the length of a side, or a relationship between two elements, for example. Park all of that information on your drawing.

Step 3—Make deductions. If a problem gives you two angles in a triangle, you can calculate the third. Always fill in anything else you can find as a matter of good test-taking habits. Sometimes deductions alone are enough to lead you to the correct answer.

Step 4—Write down relevant formulas. Geometry on the GRE is all about finding the missing piece of information. Writing down the formulas you need will help you to organize the information you have and will also help you determine which pieces you are missing. For example, if you are working with triangles and you see the word "area," automatically write down the formula for the area of a triangle. You will end up needing this formula sooner or later. This is true for any problem that involves a formula.

Step 5—Drop heights/draw lines. When taking the test, you always want to be doing, not thinking. When you get stuck on a geometry problem, first walk away and do a few other problems to distract your brain. When you come back, you need to find another way to view the problem. This is where Step 5 comes in. Try dropping the height of a triangle or parallelogram, drawing in a few extra radii in a circle, or subdividing a strange shape to make two shapes you recognize. Keep trying things! Staring at the problem isn't going to make it easier.

Here's an example:

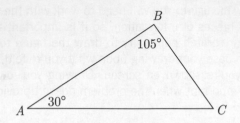

In the triangle above, if $BC = 4\sqrt{2}$, then $AB =$

○ 6

○ $4\sqrt{3}$

○ 8

○ $4\sqrt{6}$

○ 10

Step 1—Draw the figure.

Step 2—Fill in what you know. *BC* is $4\sqrt{2}$. This is a highly suspicious number. No one, not even ETS, randomly decides to make one side of a triangle include a square root. There must be a reason. What kind of triangle uses a $\sqrt{2}$?

Step 3—Make deductions. You know the third angle. It's 45°. Now you have a 45-degree angle and a $\sqrt{2}$ in the same problem. There must be a 45-45-90 triangle in here somewhere.

Step 4—Write relevant formulas. This problem doesn't call for any formulas.

Step 5—Drop heights/draw lines. Anytime you drop the height of a triangle, a right angle is formed by the intersection of the height and the base of the triangle. Look at that. There's the 45-45-90 triangle! The angle at the top is 45° too. If the hypotenuse is $4\sqrt{2}$, then each of the smaller sides is 4. Put those numbers on your drawing. On the other side there is another triangle. This one has a 30° angle and a 90° angle. You don't even have to calculate the third angle; it must be 60°. This is a 30-60-90 triangle, which means that you know the ratio of the sides. The short side opposite the 30–degree angle is 4. The long side opposite the right angle, therefore, must be 8. This is side *AB*, which is the side you were asked to find. The correct answer is (C). Your scratch paper could look like this:

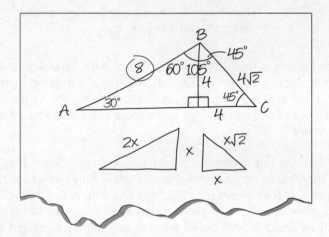

Geometry problems are often like a small piece of knitting. Once you find and tug on the loose thread, the whole thing begins to unravel. The steps are designed to tease out that loose thread.

Geometry on Quant Comp

<table>
<tr><td align="center"><u>Quantity A</u></td><td align="center"><u>Quantity B</u></td></tr>
<tr><td>The area of a square region with perimeter 20</td><td>The area of a rectangular region with perimeter 20</td></tr>
</table>

○ Quantity A is greater.

○ Quantity B is greater.

○ The two quantities are equal.

○ The relationship cannot be determined from the information given.

When solving a Quantitative Comparison with variables, always Plug In more than once. The equivalent of Plugging In more than once with a geometry question is drawing the figure more than once. Ask yourself, "Is there more than one way to draw this figure?"

You can set this problem up just like a Quant Comp Plug In. Quantity A does not change because there is only one way to draw a square. If the perimeter is 20, then one side is 5, and the area is 25. Now draw a rectangle for Quantity B and make the area as small as possible. You could have a long skinny rectangle with long sides of 9 and short sides of 1. The perimeter is 20, but the area is 9. Cross off (B) and (C). Now redraw the figure. How big can you make that area? The biggest you could make it is to make a square with sides of 5 (a square is a rectangle). The perimeter is 20, and the area is 25. Cross off (A). The answer is (D).

Your scratch paper could look something like this:

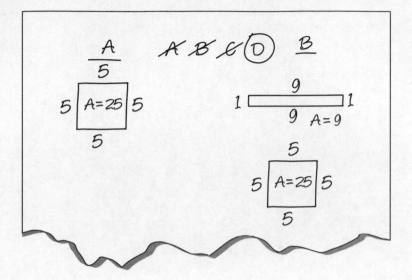

STEP 8

Ballpark the Equations

Ballpark the Equations

Many GRE math problems involve words, letters, or variables, such as *n*, *x*, or *y*, in equations. It's time to learn how to deal with those.

Solving for One Variable

Any equation with one variable can be solved by manipulating the equation. You get the variables on one side of the equation and the numbers on the other side. To do this, you can add, subtract, multiply, or divide both sides of the equation by the same number. Just remember that anything you do to one side of an equation, you have to do to the other side. Be sure to write down every step. Look at a simple example:

$$4x - 3 = 9$$

You can get rid of negatives by adding something to both sides of the equation, just as you can get rid of positives by subtracting something from both sides of the equation.

$$
\begin{array}{r}
4x - 3 = 9 \\
\underline{+3 \ +3} \\
4x \quad\ = 12
\end{array}
$$

You may already see that $x = 3$. But don't forget to write down that last step. Divide both sides of the equation by 4.

$$\frac{4x}{4} = \frac{12}{4}$$

$$x = 3$$

More Math Vocab

F.O.I.L.—F.O.I.L. stands for First, Outer, Inner, Last—the four steps of multiplication when you see two sets of parentheses. Here's an example:

$$(x + 4)(x + 3) = \overbrace{(x + 4)(x + 3)}$$

$$= (x \times x) + (x \times 3) + (4 \times x) + (4 \times 3)$$

$$= x^2 + 3x + 4x + 12$$

$$= x^2 + 7x + 12$$

This also works in the opposite direction.

Factoring—If you rewrite the expression $xy + xz$ as $x(y + z)$, you are said to be factoring the original expression. That is, you take the factor common to both terms of the original expression (x) and "pull it out." This gives you a new, "factored" version of the expression you began with. If you rewrite the expression $x(y + z)$ as $xy + xz$, you are unfactoring the original expression.

Functions—No, not real mathematical functions. On the GRE, a function is a funny-looking symbol that stands for an operation. For example, say you're told that $m \mathbin{@} n$ is equal to $\frac{m + n}{n - 1}$. What's the value of $4 \mathbin{@} 6$? Just follow directions: $\frac{4 + 6}{6 - 1}$, or $\frac{10}{5}$, or 2. Don't worry that "@" isn't a real mathematical operation; it could have been a "#" or an "&," or any other symbol. The point is to do what you are told to do.

Inequalities—Here are the symbols you need to know: $\neq$ means not equal to; $>$ means greater than; $<$ means less than; $\geq$ means greater than or equal to; $\leq$ means less than or equal to. You can manipulate any inequality in the same way you can an equation, with one important difference. For example,

$$10 - 5x > 0$$

You can solve this by subtracting 10 from both sides of the equation, and ending up with $-5x > -10$. Now you have to divide both sides by -5.

$$\frac{-5x}{-5} > \frac{-10}{-5}$$

With inequalities, any time you multiply or divide by a negative number, you have to flip the sign.

$$x < 2$$

Percent—Percent means "per 100" or "out of 100" or "divided by 100." If your friend finds a dollar and gives you 50 cents, your friend has given you 50 cents out of 100, or $\frac{50}{100}$ of a dollar, or 50% of a dollar. When you have to find exact percentages, it's much easier if you know how to translate word problems, which lets you express them as equations. Check out the "translation dictionary" on the next page.

Translation Dictionary	
Word	**Translates to**
percent	/100 (example: 40 percent translates to $\frac{40}{100}$)
is	=
of	×
what	any variable (x, k, b)
what percent	$\frac{x}{100}$

Let's look at this question:

What is 30% of 200?

First, translate it using the "dictionary" above.

$$x = \frac{30}{100} \times 200$$

Now reduce that 100 and 200, and solve for the variable, like this:

$$x = 30 \times 2$$

$$x = 60$$

So, 30% of 200 is 60.

Percent change—To find a percentage increase or decrease, first find the difference between the original number and the new number. Then, divide that by the original number, and then multiply the result by 100. In other words:

$$\text{Percent Change} = \frac{\text{Difference}}{\text{Original}} \times 100$$

For example, if you had to find the percent decrease from 4 to 3, first figure out what the difference is. The difference, or decrease, from 4 to 3 is 1.

The original number is 4. So,

$$\text{Percent Change} = \frac{\text{Difference}}{\text{Original}} \times 100$$

$$\text{Percent Change} = \frac{1}{4} \times 100$$

Percent Change = 25

So, the percent decrease from 4 to 3 is 25 percent.

Quadratic equations—Three equations that sometimes show up on the GRE. Here they are, in their factored and unfactored forms.

Factored form	Unfactored form
$x^2 - y^2 =$	$(x + y)(x - y)$
$(x + y)^2 =$	$x^2 + 2xy + y^2$
$(x - y)^2 =$	$x^2 - 2xy + y^2$

Simultaneous equations—Two algebraic equations that include the same variables. For example, what if you were told that $5x + 4y = 6$ and $4x + 3y = 5$, and asked what $x + y$ equals? To solve a set of simultaneous equations, you can usually either add them together or subtract one from the other (just remember when you subtract that everything you're subtracting needs to be made negative). Here's what you get when you add them:

$$5x + 4y = 6$$
$$+ \quad \underline{4x + 3y = 5}$$
$$9x + 7y = 11$$

A dead end. So, try subtraction.

$$\begin{array}{r} 5x + 4y = 6 \\ -4x - 3y = -5 \\ \hline x + y = 1 \end{array}$$

Eureka! The value of the expression $(x + y)$ is exactly what you're looking for.

Ballparking

Say you were asked to find 30% of 50. Before you do any math, look at the answer choices below:

- ○ 5
- ○ 15
- ○ 30
- ○ 80
- ○ 150

Whatever 30% of 50 is, it must be less than 50, right? So any answer choice greater than 50 cannot be correct. That means you should eliminate both 80 and 150 right off the bat, without doing any math. You can also eliminate 30, if you think about it. Half, or 50 percent, of 50 is 25, so 30 percent must be less than 25. Congratulations, you've just eliminated three out of five answer choices without doing any math.

What you've done here is known as Ballparking. Ballparking will help you eliminate answer choices and increase your odds of zeroing in on ETS's answer. Remember to eliminate any answer choice that is "out of the ballpark" by crossing them off on your scratch paper (remember, you'll be writing down A, B, C, D, E for each question).

Charts

Ballparking will also help you on the few chart questions that every GRE Math section will have. You should Ballpark whenever you see the word "approximately" in a question, whenever the answer choices are far apart in value, and whenever you start to answer a question and you justifiably say to yourself, "This is going to take a lot of calculation!"

To help you Ballpark, here are a few percents and their fractional equivalents:

1%	=	$\frac{1}{100}$
10%	=	$\frac{1}{10}$
20%	=	$\frac{1}{5}$
25%	=	$\frac{1}{4}$
$33\frac{1}{3}\%$	=	$\frac{1}{3}$
40%	=	$\frac{2}{5}$
50%	=	$\frac{1}{2}$
60%	=	$\frac{3}{5}$
$66\frac{2}{3}\%$	=	$\frac{2}{3}$
75%	=	$\frac{3}{4}$
80%	=	$\frac{4}{5}$
100%	=	$\frac{1}{1}$
200%	=	$\frac{2}{1}$

If, on a chart question, you were asked to find 9.6 percent of 21.4, you could Ballpark by using 10% as a "friendlier" percentage and 20 as a "friendlier" number. 10% of 20 is 2. That's all you need to do to answer most chart questions.

Try Ballparking on a real chart. Keep in mind that while general charts display the information they want you to see to make the information easier to understand, ETS constructs charts to *hide* the information you need to know to make that information *difficult* to understand. So read all titles and small print, to make sure you understand what the charts are conveying.

**Nationwide Survey of Ice Cream Preferences
in 1975 and in 1985, by Flavor**

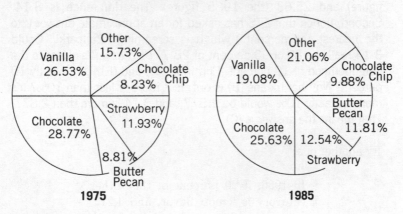

1975　　　　　　　　　　　　　**1985**

Looking over these charts, notice that they are for 1975 and 1985, and that all you know are percentages. There are no total numbers for the survey, and because the percentages are pretty "ugly," you can anticipate doing a lot of Ballparking to answer the questions.

Try the following example.

> To the nearest one percent, what
> percentage decrease in popularity occurred
> for chocolate from 1975 to 1985 ?
>
> ○ 9%
> ○ 10%
> ○ 11%
> ○ 89%
> ○ 90%

First, you need to find the difference between 28.77 (the 1975 figure) and 25.63 (the 1985 figure). The difference is 3.14. Second, notice that ETS has asked for an approximate answer ("to the nearest one percent") which is screaming "Ballpark!" Could 3.14 really be 89 or 90 percent of 28.77? No way; it's closer to the neighborhood of 10 percent. Eliminate (D) and (E). Is it exactly 10 percent? No; that means (B) is out. Is it more or less than 10%? It's more—exactly 10% would be 2.877, and 3.14 is more than 2.877. That means the answer is (C).

Try another one:

> In 1985, if 20 percent of the "other"
> category is lemon flavor, and 4,212
> people surveyed preferred lemon, then
> how many people were surveyed?
>
> ○   1,000
> ○   10,000
> ○   42,120
> ○   100,000
> ○ 1,000,000

The first piece of information you have is a percentage of a percentage. The percentage of people who preferred lemon in 1985 is equal to 20% of 21.06%. Make sure you see that before you go on. Now, notice that the numbers in the answer choices are very widely separated—they aren't consecutive integers. If you can just get in the ballpark, the answer will be obvious.

Rather than try to use 21.06%, we'll call it 20%. And rather than use 4,212, use 4,000. The question is now: "20% of 20% of *what* is 4,000?" So, using translation, your equation looks like this:

$$\frac{20}{100} \times \frac{20}{100} \times x = 4,000$$

Do a little reducing.

$$\frac{1}{5} \times \frac{1}{5} \times x = 4,000$$

$$\frac{1}{25} \times x = 4,000$$

$$x = 100,000$$

That means the answer is (D).

Get Organized When

Doing Arithmetic

STEP 9

Get Organized When Doing Arithmetic

Get Organized When Doing Arithmetic

Questions involving ratios or averages can seem daunting at first. The math involved in these problems, however, generally involves little more than basic arithmetic. The trick to these problems is understanding how to organize your information. Learning the transition words and setups for each of these problems can take a four-minute brain teaser and turn it into a 45-second piece of cake.

Averages

Imagine you are asked to find the average (arithmetic mean) of three numbers, 3, 7, and 8. This is not a difficult problem. Simply add the three together to get the total. Divide by three, the number of things, to get the average. All average problems involve three basic pieces:

- Total: 18

- Number of things: 3

- Average: 6

It is virtually assured that ETS will never give you a list of numbers and ask you for the average. That would be too easy. They will, however, always give you two out of these three pieces, and it is your job to find the third. That's where the Average Pie comes in. The minute you see the word "average" on a problem, draw your pie on your scratch paper.

Transition Word: "Average"

Response: Draw an Average Pie on your scratch paper.

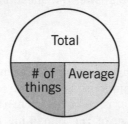

Here's how you would fill it in.

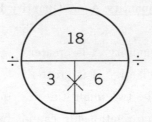

As previously stated, you won't be asked to find the average of a list of numbers. On the test, they will always give you two out of the three pieces of information you'll need to find the average. Just draw your pie, fill in what you know, and it becomes easy to find the missing piece. Here's how it works.

The line in the middle means *divide*. If you have the total and the number of things, just divide and you get the average ($18 \div 3 = 6$). If you have the total and the average, just divide and you get the number of things ($18 \div 6 = 3$). If you have the average and the number of things, simply multiply and you get the total ($6 \times 3 = 18$). As you will see, the key to most average questions is finding the total.

The benefit of the Average Pie is that you simply have to plug the information from the question into the Average Pie and then complete the pie. Doing so will automatically give you all the information you need to answer the question.

Try this question:

> The average (arithmetic mean) of a set of 6 numbers is 28. If a certain number, y, is removed from the set, the average of the remaining numbers in the set is 24.

Quantity A	Quantity B
y	48

○ Quantity A is greater.

○ Quantity B is greater.

○ The two quantities are equal.

○ The relationship cannot be determined from the information given.

The minute you see the word "average," make your pie. If you see the word "average" a second time, make a second pie. Start with the first bite-sized piece, "The average of a set of 6 numbers is 28." Draw your pie and fill it in. With the average and the number of things you can calculate the total, like this:

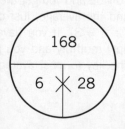

Take your next piece of the problem, "If a certain number, y, is removed from the set, the average of the remaining numbers in the set is 24." There's the word "average" again, so make another pie. Again, you have the number of things (5, because one number was removed from our set) and the average, 24, so you can calculate the total, like this:

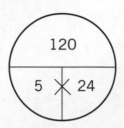

The total for all six numbers is 168. When you take a number out, the total for the remaining five is 120. The number you removed, therefore, must be $168 - 120 = 48$. $y = 48$. The answer is (C).

Ratios

When working with fractions, decimals, and percentages, you are working with a part to a whole relationship. The fraction $\frac{3}{5}$ means 3 parts out of a total of 5, and 20% means 20 parts out of every 100. A ratio, on the other hand, is a part to a part relationship. Lemons and limes in a ratio of 1 to 4 means that you have one lemon for every four limes. If you make an Average Pie every time you see the word "average," you should make a Ratio Box every time you see the word "ratio."

Here's an actual GRE problem:

> In a club with 35 members, the ratio of men to women is 2 to 3 among the members. How many men belong to the club?
>
> ○ 2
> ○ 5
> ○ 7
> ○ 14
> ○ 21

The problem says, "the ratio of men to women…." As soon as you see that, make your box. It could look like this:

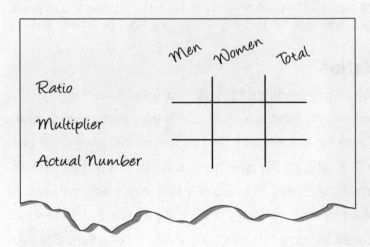

In the top line of the box, list the items that make up your ratio, in this case, men and women. The last column is always for the total. In the second row of the box, fill in your ratio of 2 to 3 under Men and Women, respectively. The total is 5. This doesn't mean that there are actually 2 men and 3 women in the club. This just means that for every 5 members of this club, 2 of them will be men and 3 of them will be women. The actual number of members, you're told in the problem, is 35. This goes in the bottom right cell under Total. With this single number in the bottom row you can figure out the rest. To get from 5 to 35, you need to multiply by 7. The multiplier remains constant across the ratio, so fill a 7 in all three cells of the third row, next to the word "multiplier." You now know that the actual number of men in the club is 14, just as the actual number of women is 21. The answer is (D). Here's what your completed Ratio Box could look like:

	Men	Women	Total
Ratio	2	3	5
	×	×	×
Multiplier	7	7	7
	=	=	=
Actual Number	14	21	35

The fraction of the club that is male is $\frac{14}{35}$. If you reduce this, you get $\frac{2}{5}$. The percentage of members who are female is $\frac{3}{5}$, or 60%.

Median/Mode/Range

"Median" means the number in the middle, like the median strip on a highway. In the set of numbers 2, 2, 4, 5, 9, the median is "4" because it's the one in the middle. If the set had an even number of elements, let's say: 2, 3, 4, 6, the median is the average of the two numbers in the middle or, in this case, 3.5. That's it. There's not much that's interesting about the word "median." There are only two ways they can trick you with a median question. One is to give you a set with an even number of elements. You've mastered that one. The other is to give you a set of numbers which are out of order. If you see the word "median," therefore, find a bunch of numbers and put them in order.

"Mode" simply means the number that shows up the most. In the set 2, 2, 4, 5, 9, the mode is 2. That's all there is to mode. If no number shows up more than another, then the set has no mode.

"Range" is even easier. It is the difference between the biggest number in a set and the smallest. In other words, find the smallest number and subtract it from the biggest number.

Look at this problem:

> If in the set of numbers {20, 14, 19, 12, 17, 20, 24} v equals the mean, w equals the median, x equals the mode, and y equals the range, which of the following is true?
>
> ○ $v < w < x < y$
>
> ○ $v < x < w < y$
>
> ○ $y < v < w < x$
>
> ○ $y < v < x < w$
>
> ○ $w < y < v < x$

In this question you're asked to find the mean, the median, the mode, and the range of a set of numbers. The minute you see the word "median," you know what to do. Put the numbers in order: 12, 14, 17, 19, 20, 20, 24. Do this on your scratch paper, not in your head, and while you're at it, list A, B, C, D, and E so that you have something to eliminate. The minute you put the numbers in order, three out of the four elements you are asked to find should become clear. The range, 12, is equal to the smallest number in this case, so y should be the element at the far left of the series. Cross off (A), (B), and (E). The average will be somewhere in the middle. Without doing some calculations, it's not clear if it is larger than the median (19) or smaller, so skip to the mode. The mode is 20 and larger than the median and certainly larger than the mean. Variable x should be the last element in the series. Cross off (D). The correct answer is (C). Always remember that the answer choices are part of the question. Often it is far easier to find and eliminate wrong answers than it is to find the correct ones.

Rates and Proportions

Rates are really just proportions. Similar to ratios and averages, the basic math is straightforward, but the difficult part is organizing the information. Actually, organizing the information is the whole trick. Set up all rates like a proportion and make sure you label the top and bottom of your proportion. Look at an actual problem below.

Stan drives at an average speed of 60 miles per hour from Town A to Town B, a distance of 150 miles. Ollie drives at an average speed of 50 miles per hour from Town C to Town B, a distance of 120 miles.

Quantity A	Quantity B
Amount of time Stan spends driving	Amount of time Ollie spends driving

○ Quantity A is greater.

○ Quantity B is greater.

○ The two quantities are equal.

○ The relationship cannot be determined from the information given.

In this problem you are asked to compare two separate rates, each consisting of miles (distance) and hours (time). Start with Stan. Stan's speed is 60 mph, which is to say that he drives 60 miles every 1 hour. You're asked to find how many hours it will take him to travel 150 miles. Just set it up as a proportion, like this:

$$\frac{miles}{hours} \quad \overset{Stan}{\frac{60}{1}} = \frac{150}{x} \quad \overset{Ollie}{\frac{50}{1}} = \frac{120}{x}$$

Now you can compare miles to miles and hours to hours. There is an x in the second space for hours because you don't yet know how many hours it's going to take Stan. The nice thing about this setup is that you can always cross-multiply to find the missing piece. If $60x = 150$, then $x = 2.5$. This means that it took Stan 2.5 hours to drive 150 miles (at a rate of 60 miles per hour).

Now try Ollie. The setup is the same. Ollie drives 50 miles for every one hour. To find out how many hours he needs to drive 120 miles, just cross-multiply. If $50x = 120$, then $x = 2.4$. This means that it took Ollie 2.4 hours to drive 120 miles (at a rate of 50 miles per hour). Quantity A is Stan, so the correct answer is (A).

Arithmetic Summary

Here are a list of transition words and what you should do when you see them in the Quantitative section of the exam.

Transition Word	Response
Average	Draw an Average Pie.
Ratio	Draw a Ratio Box.
Median	Find a bunch of numbers and put them in order.
Mode	Find the number that appears the most often.
Range	Subtract the smallest from the biggest.
Rate	Set up a proportion; label top and bottom.

Plan Before Writing Your Essays

Plan Before Writing Your Essays

The Issue Essay

Your issue essay will be read by two graders, and each will assign a score from 1 to 6, based on how well you do the following:

- follow the instructions of the prompt

- consider the complexities of the issue or argument

- effectively organize and develop your ideas

- support your position with relevant examples

- control the elements of written English

The graders will be judging your essays on three basic criteria: the quality of your thinking, the quality of your organizing, and the quality of your writing. The two graders scores will be averaged, and the two essay scores will be averaged. Quarter points are rounded up in the student's favor.

An essay with well-chosen examples, clear organization, and decent use of standard written English is automatically in the top half, guaranteeing a score of at least a 4. If any one of those categories is particularly strong, then your score goes from a 4 to a 5. If two of them are particularly strong, your score goes up to a 6. On the other hand, if any one of those three elements is missing, no matter what's going on with the other two, you are automatically in the bottom half. Since they will be judging your essays based upon these three criteria, you need a process that gives each its due.

You will be given a topic of general interest. The topic will be general enough that it is accessible to any test taker anywhere. ETS could never ask a question about, say, *Hamlet*, because this would advantage one group of test takers over another. Topics, therefore, tend to be about loss, growth, education, the role of government, individuals and society, etc. In fact, all topics you might see are posted right now on **www.ets.org/gre,** on the "Published Topic Pools for the Analytical Writing Measure" page.

Your job is to formulate an opinion about this topic and craft a convincing an argument in support of your opinion. You will need to support your argument with specific examples. You can choose to agree, disagree, or even modify the issue topic, just as long as you stay on topic.

Step 1: Think

One of the most common mistakes that students make is they write their essays based upon the first two or three examples they come up with. Rarely are these the best or even the most interesting examples. Rarely do they show any development, and often they are the same examples that everyone else comes up with. ETS graders are judging you on the quality of your thinking, so take time to think.

Define the Topic

Essay topics typically fall into one of three general categories. There are extreme statements, wishy-washy statements, and open-ended statements. Your first job is to figure out what it means to agree or disagree with the statement. To agree with an extreme statement is to take an extreme position. This has the benefit of a very clear thesis statement, but may be difficult to defend. It is often easier to disagree with an extreme statement. To agree with a wishy-washy statement is usually pretty easy. Just say, "Sure, this is often true. Here are some examples...." To disagree with a wishy-washy statement is to take an extreme position. You must show that the statement is never true or always true. It is often easier to agree with a wishy-washy statement.

Brainstorm

Once you have defined the topic (this should take a minute or less), it's time to brainstorm. Your job, at this stage, is to push your thinking as far as it can go. Your job, whether you agree with the topic or not, is to come up with at least four "agree" examples, and four "disagree" examples. Quantity and variety are more important than quality at this point. On your scratch paper, draw a "T." on the left, write, "I agree," and on the right write "I disagree."

Your scratch paper could look like this:

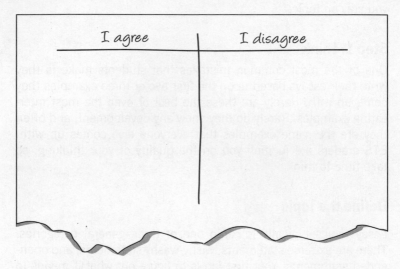

Argue From a Position of Strength

Topics are always general enough so that they are accessible to all test takers, no matter who they are or where they're taking the test. This means that you can apply them to just about any area of expertise or experience. The place to start is with your own areas of expertise. How is the topic true for you? Could it apply to your field of study? Could it apply to your school? Is it true for your company? Go into the exam prepared to talk about the things you know best. What was your major in school? Where do you work now? What books have you recently read or papers have you

Crash Course for the GRE

have recently written? Essays written from an area of strength are always easier to write and far more convincing. It's always easier to talk about things you know well, and when you do, you will come across as an expert, because you are.

When your brainstorm runs dry, use this checklist:

---

yourself, friends, family, school, city, country, company, species, old/young, history, science, literature

---

This should push your thinking in new directions. How is the topic true for the very old or the very young? What about at the species level? Could it occur in another species? Can it be true for an individual but also a country or company?

The first three examples you come up with are likely to be very similar. They might be three major figures in history, for example. One of those examples might be good, but the second and third don't advance your argument. Write them down as part of your brainstorm, but make sure to push your thinking into other areas. Each example you choose should have a specific job to do. They are the legs of the argument you are creating. An essay that shows development, or quality thinking, will look at the topic from multiple angles. Each example will bring something new to the argument.

Many students are worried about time at this stage. First, you are being judged on the quality of your thinking, so you cannot ignore this step. Next, a good brainstorm and a good outline will help you to be more efficient and more focused when you write. And lastly, thinking while you write is dangerous. Essays written on the fly often have a lack of focus and structure. When you are trying to think and work at the same time, you distract your brain while you're writing leading to embarrassing mistakes in grammar, punctuation, and diction.

The other thing to keep in mind is that the ETS website states, The GRE readers scoring your response are not looking for a "right" answer—in fact, as far as they are concerned, there is no correct position to take. Instead, the readers are evaluating the skill with which you address the specific instructions and articulate and develop an argument to support your evaluation of the issue. This means that you are free to approach the topic from any angle you want. It also means that you can focus on one particular area or application of the topic.

Step 2: Organize

Most students come up with a point of view and then rack their brains for the perfect examples to support it. They will often come up with that perfect example, but usually it doesn't happen until hours after the exam. The best way to perfectly connect your examples and your thesis statement is to select your examples first.

Some essay instructions will be relatively straightforward, such as "Present a point of view and support it with well-chosen examples." Other instructions may be more specific, such as "Present your position on the issue and describe a situation in which the implementation of your recommendation would not be advantageous." Paying close attention to the instructions you have been given, craft your point of view by selecting your three strongest examples. Be sure that each of your examples performs a specific and distinct job in support of your position.

Once you have selected your best examples, write a thesis statement to accommodate your examples. In this way, you will always have the perfect examples for your thesis statement because the examples came first! On your scratch paper, jot down your thesis, and underneath it, list your three examples in the order in which you plan to use them. Next to each example, jot down just a few words to remind yourself why you've chosen that example. These words will prove why the example is a perfect illustration of your thesis.

You now have three interesting examples that show different perspectives on the issue: a thesis statement, which is perfectly supported by your examples; a clear, well-organized outline for your essay; and even the makings of a topic sentence for each of your supporting paragraphs. Not only are you now ready to write, but when it comes time to write, you can focus just on your writing. You don't have to be distracted by thinking about where your essay is going next. You've got a good clear plan: Stick to it. Your essay at this point is 60 percent done. You have the majority of your introductory paragraph and the beginning of the topic sentences for each of your supporting paragraphs. All you need to do is explain each of your examples in greater detail, come up with a conclusion, and you're done. It's time to start writing.

Step 3: Write

When it comes to writing, there are two things your essay *must* have and a handful of things it *might* have to get credit for good writing.

Must Have:

- **Topic sentences**—A topic sentence announces the subject and or point of each supporting paragraph. It could be quite literal such as "_____ is an example of why [restate your thesis]," or something more nuanced. Use your topic sentence to link each example to your thesis and to indicate to the reader the point you would like each example to make. Make it easy for your reader to get your point and the direction in which you are going. The harder your reader has to work to find your point, the lower your score will go. It does not pay to be overly subtle when your reader will spend only one to two minutes on your essay.

- **Transitions**—Transitions give your essay flow. They indicate changes in scale, direction, or perspective and help the reader get from one paragraph to the next. It might be just a few words attached to your topic sentence or a whole sentence. If you are changing direction, for example, simply saying "on the other hand" or "in contrast" might be sufficient. If you are changing scale or perspective, you might say "When viewed from the perspective of a _____" or "What is true for an individual is equally true for a _____. For example..."

Might Have:

- **Specifics**—When you argue from a position of strength, specifics should be easy. Use names, dates, places, and any other relevant details. The details bring an example to life and make you sound like an expert.

- **Quotes**—In many ways, a quote is like the ultimate specific. You can't always use quotes, but if you have a good one and you can drop it comfortably into your essay, it's quite impressive.

- **Big words**—Big words used correctly always score points. They are a way to distinguish yourself from the other writers. They are also something that can be prepared in advance. Generate a list of impressive words that you know well and look for places to use them.

- **Analogies**—To say that censorship, for example, is a double-edged sword may be a bit clichéd, but it is also a terrific way to set up an argument that has two sides. Using a good metaphor is like tucking a snazzy silk handkerchief in your breast pocket. It's not necessary or even common, but if you can pull it off, it raises the whole ensemble to another level.

- **Length**—Length counts. Statistically speaking, longer essays score better. That means beefing up your typing skills. If you have time, drop in a fourth example or add a few more details to each of your first three examples.

- **Rhetorical questions**—Does anything sound more professorial in an essay than the occasional rhetorical question? It is a rhetorical flourish that is rarely used but particularly effective for this type of essay. It allows you to speak directly to your reader and represents a sophisticated way of jumping into a topic that most writers never consider.

- **Commands**—Use them. They will grab the reader's attention. It is a bold style of writing that few people use.

The Argument Essay

For the issue essay, your job is to craft your own argument. For the argument essay, your job is the opposite. You will be given someone else's argument, and you must break it down and assess it. In some ways, this is not difficult. The argument you're given will be filled with some pretty obvious flaws.

Here's an example of the type of prompts you will see for your argument essay:

The following appeared in a memorandum from the regional manager of the Taste of Italy restaurant chain.

"After the first month of service, the new restaurant in the Flatplains Mall, which uses the Chipless brand of wine glasses, has reported a far lower rate of breakage than our other restaurants that use the Elegance brand. Since servers and a bartenders at all of our restaurants frequently report that breakage is a result of the type of wineglass, and the customers at the Flatplains Mall restaurant seem to like the Chipless style of glasses, we should switch all of our restaurants over to the Chipless brand."

Instructions

The argument text will be followed by a brief series of instructions. You may be asked for ways to strengthen an argument, find alternative explanations for an argument (weaken), discuss questions to be asked about the argument (identify premise and assumptions), discuss evidence needed to evaluate the argument, and so on. All instructions will ask you to work with the basic parts of an argument in some way. No matter what, you must be prepared to identify the parts of an argument and different types of argument and explain how they all work.

Breaking Down the Argument

There are three basic parts to any argument: the conclusion, the premises, and the assumptions.

The Conclusion

The conclusion is the point of the argument. The author is trying to convince you of something. That something is the conclusion. Typically, the conclusion will be stated, and it is often indicated by words such as "therefore" or "in conclusion." It is possible, however, for a conclusion to be implied.

The Premises

Once you identify the conclusion, ask yourself, "Why?" The answers to that question that are stated in the argument are the premises. They are always stated. There will be a few of them. They are the evidence cited to support the conclusion.

The Assumptions

Assumptions are never stated. They link the conclusion to the premises, and there are hundreds of assumptions. When you brainstorm an argument, the assumptions are what you are looking for. They are all of the things that have to be true in order for the conclusion to be true.

When you begin to break down an argument, you will want to use the formal language of arguments. First, identify the conclusion, then the premises, and finally, the assumptions.

Types of Arguments

There are some types of arguments that you will see frequently. Once you identify the type of argument, spotting the assumption is easy.

Causal: A Causes B

A causal argument assumes a cause-and-effect relationship between two events. For example, *employee turnover is up because salaries are down*. The conclusion is that lower salaries caused employee turnover to go up. To weaken a causal argument, you need to point out other potential causes for a particular event. Perhaps employee turnover is up because of a change in management or other policies. Perhaps there is another company offering better jobs. To strengthen a causal argument, you need to show that other potential causes are unlikely.

Sampling or Statistical: A = A, B, C

In these arguments the author assumes that a particular group represents an entire population. For example, *nine out of ten doctors surveyed prefer a particular brand of chewing gum*. The conclusion is that 90 percent of all doctors prefer this brand of chewing gum. Is that true? To weaken this argument, you need to show that the people in the group surveyed don't represent the whole population. Perhaps they surveyed doctors at the chewing gum's annual shareholder meeting. Perhaps they surveyed doctors in the city where the chewing gum has its headquarters. To strengthen this argument, you need to show that the sample population is, in fact, representative of the whole.

Analogy: A = B

Analogy arguments claim that what is true for one group is also true for another. For example, *football players like a particular brand of cleats, so soccer players should too*. The conclusion is that soccer players should like this brand of cleats. Why? Because football players like them. This is the premise. The main assumption is that soccer players should like the same thing as football players. Is this true? To weaken analogy arguments you need to show that the two groups are not at all analogous. Perhaps football players prefer cleats that offer foot protection, while soccer players want ones that mold to the foot. To strengthen these arguments, you must show that the two groups are quite similar indeed (at least in their shoe choice).

Crafting Your Argument Essay

The overall process for crafting your essay will be the same as it is for the issue essay. Invariably, you will have to follow the approach dictated by your instructions. But no matter what, you will need to identify and address weaknesses in the argument. Throughout your essay you should use the language of argument. This means naming conclusions as conclusions, sampling arguments as sampling arguments, premises as premises, and assumptions as assumptions.

Thinking

Begin by identifying your conclusion and then identify the major premises upon which it rests. For each premise note the type of reasoning used (sampling, causal, and so on), and the flaws associated with that type of reasoning. This is as much brainstorming as you will need.

Organizing

Rank the premises by the size of their flaws. Start with the most egregious and work your way down. The outline of your essay will look something like the following:

- The author's conclusion is *z*. It is faulty and more research/ information is needed before the suggested action is taken.

- The first and biggest flaw is premise *y*. It's possible that it is true, but it rests upon the following assumptions. Can we really make these assumptions? What about these alternative assumptions?

- Even if we assume *y* to be the case, there is premise *x*. Premise *x* draws an analogy between these two groups and assumes that they are interchangeable. Can we really make this assumption? What about these alternative assumptions?

- Even if we assume *x* to be true, there is also *w*. *w* is a sampling argument, but the author not only has not proven the sample to be representative, but he/she also points out that this may not be the case! Perhaps, as noted, blah, blah, blah.

In conclusion, this argument is incomplete and rests upon too many questionable assumptions. To improve this argument, the author needs to show *a, b,* and *c,* before the building is to be torn down (or the company is to change tactics, the school is to reorganize its curriculum, and so on).

Writing

Feel free to have fun with this essay. Reading essays can get pretty boring, and a smart, funny critique of a faulty argument can be a welcomed break for your reader. You might say, "If I were the president of company *x*, I would fire my marketing director for wasting my time with such a poorly researched plan." It's okay to have personality as long as you get the analysis of the argument done at the same time.

For a more in-depth look at the techniques for the argument essay and some sample essays, check out our latest *Cracking the GRE* book. Also check out the *ScoreItNow!*™ Online Writing Practice service available for purchase on the ETS website.

PART III
Drills

Verbal Drill 1

1. Children, after more than a generation of television, have become "hasty viewers"; as a result, if the camera lags, the attention of these young viewers _____.

   ○ expands

   ○ starts

   ○ alternates

   ○ wanes

   ○ clarifies

2. Certainly the architect's _____ is not due to his promotional skills, indeed, he isolated himself from everything that could disturb his work.

   ○ proficiency

   ○ temperament

   ○ prominence

   ○ superiority

   ○ reticence

3. The violinist's (i)＿＿＿＿＿ performance, coupled with the (ii)＿＿＿＿＿ cadences of the renowned composer's music, roused the audience to a standing ovation.

Blank (i)	Blank (ii)
prosaic	soporific
hackneyed	mellifluous
virtuosic	insipid

4. Research into early childhood education, which advocates providing toddlers as young as two or three with a plenitude of intellectually stimulating activities, has produced (i)＿＿＿＿＿ results. Such findings, however, have failed to (ii)＿＿＿＿＿ many parents from enrolling their children in such unproven programs.

Blank (i)	Blank (ii)
conclusive	disabuse
ambiguous	dissuade
auspicious	distinguish

5. Classical economics views humans as rational, pragmatic creatures who nonetheless seek to maximize their own (i)_____. Veblen, in contrast, depicts humans as (ii)_____ beings, pursuing social status with (iii)_____ regard for their own happiness.

Blank (i)	Blank (ii)	Blank (iii)
melancholy	irrational	sporadic
bliss	pugnacious	scant
discord	mundane	stoic

6. While (i)_____ has always been a problem in college classrooms, some feared the availability of online resources would cause the problem to (ii)_____. However, educators have been able to take advantage of Internet tools to check their students' work against any material online and thus (iii)_____ that their students are truly submitting their own work and not simply copying from a website.

Blank (i)	Blank (ii)	Blank (iii)
tardiness	proliferate	ensure
abstraction	descend	rebut
plagiarism	delineate	neglect

7. The skill level of medieval stoneworkers clearly exceeds that of their modern counterparts. A trade journal recently published the results of a decade-long survey of master stonemasons in Europe. According to the report, a clear majority of respondents noted that medieval cathedrals exhibit a consistently higher level of craftsmanship in their stonework than do similar edifices built in the last hundred years.

Which of the following, if true, would most seriously weaken the above argument?

○ The stonemason's main tools are virtually unchanged since the Middle Ages.

○ The stonework in cathedrals is typical of that in surviving medieval structures.

○ Most medieval cathedrals are significantly larger than modern stone edifices.

○ The practice of apprenticeship had declined significantly since the Middle Ages.

○ Higher quality stonework is less likely to fall into disrepair and be destroyed.

Questions 8–11 refer to the following passage.

Although the study of women's history has only been developed as an academic discipline in the last twenty years, it is not the case that the current wave of feminist activity is Line the first in which interest in women's past was manifest. From 5 its very beginnings, the nineteenth-century English women's movement sought to expand existing knowledge of the activities and achievements of women in the past. At the same time, like its American counterpart, the English women's movement had a powerful sense of its own historic importance and of its 10 relationship to wider social and political change.

Nowhere is this sense of the historical importance—and of the historical connections between the women's movement and other social and political developments—more evident than in Ray Strachey's classic account of the movement, *The* 15 *Cause.* "The true history of the Women's Movement," Strachey argues, "is the whole history of the nineteenth century." The women's movement was part of the broad sweep of liberal and progressive reform that was transforming society. Strachey emphasized this connection between the women's movement 20 and the broader sweep of history by highlighting the influence of the Enlightenment and the Industrial Revolution on it. The protest made by the women's movement at the confinement and injustices faced by women was, in Strachey's view, part of the liberal attack on traditional prejudices and injustice. 25 This critique of women's confinement was supplemented by the demand for recognition of women's roles in the public, particularly the philanthropic realm. Indeed, it was the criticism of the limitations faced by women on the one hand, and their establishment of a new public role on the other hand, 30 that provided the core of the movement, determining also its form: its organization around campaigns for legal, political, and social reform.

Strachey's analysis was a very illuminating one, nowhere more so than in her insistence that, despite their differences and even antipathy to each other, both the radical Mary Wollstonecraft and evangelical Hannah More need to be seen as forerunners of mid-Victorian feminism. At the same time, she omitted some issues that now seem crucial to any discussion of the context of Victorian feminism. Where Strachey pictured a relatively fixed image of domestic women throughout the first half of the nineteenth century, recent historical and literary works suggest that this image was both complex and unstable. The establishment of a separate domestic sphere for women was but one aspect of the enormous change in sexual and familial relationships that was occurring from the late eighteenth through the mid-nineteenth century. These changes were accompanied by both anxiety and uncertainty and by the constant articulation of women's duties in a new social world.

8. The primary purpose of the passage is to

○ present an overview of the economic changes that led to the English women's movement

○ evaluate a view of the English women's movement as presented in a literary work

○ describe the social and political context of the women's movement in England

○ offer a novel analysis of England's reaction to the women's movement

○ profile several of the women who were instrumental in the success of the English women's movement

9. The author includes Strachey's claim that "the true history of the Women's Movement...is the whole history of the nineteenth century" (lines 15–16) in order to emphasize

○ Strachey's belief that the advancement of women's rights was the most significant development of its century

○ the importance Strachey attributes to the women's movement in bringing about the Enlightenment

○ Strachey's awareness of the interconnection of the women's movement and other societal changes in the 1800s

○ Strachey's contention that the women's movement, unlike other social and political developments of the time, actually transformed society

○ Strachey's argument that the nineteenth century must play a role in any criticism of the limitations of women

10. While the author acknowledges Strachey's importance in the study of women's history, she faults Strachey for

○ focusing her study on the legal and political reform enacted by the women's movement

○ oversimplifying her conception of the social condition of women prior to the reforms of the women's movement

○ failing to eliminate the anachronistic idea of "women's duty" from her articulation of nineteenth-century feminism

○ omitting Mary Wollstonecraft and Hannah More from her discussion of important influences in feminism

○ recommending a static and domestic social role for women following the women's movement

11. Which of the following, if true, would most weaken the author's assertion about the similarity between the English and American women's movements?

○ The English and American women's movements took place in very different sociohistorical climates.

○ The English women's movement began almost a century before the American women's movement.

○ The English women's movement excluded men, while the American women's movement did not.

○ Few members of the English women's movement were aware of the impact it would have on society.

○ Many participants in the English women's movement continued to perform traditional domestic roles.

12. Though not completely _____ , the newest edition of the book is certainly very different from any previously published version.

☐ familiar

☐ unrecognizable

☐ answerable

☐ legitimate

☐ reworked

☐ gentrified

13. Merzon's _____ behavior convinced his colleagues that he had ulterior motives.

☐ inconspicuous

☐ furtive

☐ overt

☐ unorthodox

☐ predictable

☐ surreptitious

14. With its refined interiors and amply stocked reading room, the hotel catered to the most _____ of travelers.

☐ philistine

☐ urbane

☐ cosmopolitan

☐ uncouth

☐ grandiloquent

☐ pretentious

15. By far not the most _____ of men, Wilbert nonetheless enjoyed renown that was unimpeded by his inherent irascibility.

☐ loquacious

☐ pedantic

☐ amiable

☐ garrulous

☐ affable

☐ stentorian

16. Select the sentence in the passage that best supports the author's main idea.

It is hard from our modern perspective to imagine that theater has the power to influence politics, yet the plays of pre-republican Ireland did just that. Crippled by the censorious English rule and muted by population migration, Irish culture had fallen into an almost irrevocable decline by the second half of the 19th Century. A group of Dublin intellectuals and writers, calling themselves the Gaelic League, formed a society dedicated to the revival of Irish culture. Among its illustrious members, the League boasted William Butler Yeats, J.M. Synge, Sean O'Casey, and Lady Gregory. The founding of the Abbey Theatre and the production of Irish plays were directly responsible for the resurgence of interest in Irish language and culture, culminating in the European Union's decision in 2005 to make Irish an official language of that body.

Questions 17–20 refer to the following passage.

Following the discovery in 1895 that malaria is carried by *Anopheles* mosquitoes, governments around the world set out to eradicate those insect vectors. In Europe, the rela-
Line tion between the malarial agent, protozoan blood parasites of
5 the genus Plasmodium, and the vector mosquito, *Anopheles maculipennis*, seemed at first inconsistent. In some locali-ties the mosquito was abundant but malaria rare or absent, while in others the reverse was true. In 1934 the problem was solved. Entomologists discovered that *A. maculipennis* is not a
10 single species but a group of at least seven.

In outward appearance, the adult mosquitoes seem almost identical, but in fact they are marked by a host of distinctive biological traits, some of which prevent them from hybridizing. Some of the species distinguished by these traits were found to
15 feed on human blood and thus to carry the malarial parasites. Once identified, the dangerous members of the *A. maculipennis* complex could be targeted and eradicated.

17. Which of the following best describes the reason that scientists were initially perplexed at the discovery that malaria was spread by *Anopheles* mosquitoes?

○ Scientists had evidence that malaria was carried by the protozoan blood parasite Plasmodium.

○ Scientists felt that because so many species of *Anopheles* existed, they could not be carriers.

○ Scientists were unable to find a direct correlation between *Anopheles* density and frequency of malaria occurrence.

○ Scientists knew that many species of *Anopheles* mosquito did not feed on human blood.

○ Scientists believed that the *Anopheles* mosquito could not be host to the parasite Plasmodium.

18. In the context in which it appears, "host" (line 12) most nearly means

○ scarcity

○ sacrament

○ multitude

○ organism receiving a transplant

○ organism supporting a parasite

19. It can be inferred from the passage that a mosquito becomes a carrier of malaria when

○ it ingests the blood of a human being infected with malaria

○ it lives in regions where malaria is widespread

○ it consumes blood from a protozoan malarial agent

○ it has extended contact with other insect vectors

○ it is spawned in Plasmodium-infested localities

20. The bolded text plays which of the following roles in the passage?

○ It provides evidence to weaken the author's main point.

○ It provides evidence to strengthen the author's main point.

○ It clarifies the importance of solving a paradox expressed in the passage.

○ It gives the resolution to a paradox expressed in the passage.

○ It explains why a paradox expressed in the passage resisted easy resolution.

Verbal Drill 2

1. Many scholars feel that historical events can be seen
   as _____; what one group sees as peacekeeping,
   another group might see as subjugation.

   - ○ academic
   - ○ portentous
   - ○ paradoxical
   - ○ trifling
   - ○ bellicose

2. The American public venerates medical researchers
   because the researchers make frequent discoveries of
   tremendous humanitarian consequence; however, the
   daily routines of scientists are largely made up of
   result verification and statistical analysis, making their
   occupation seem _____.

   - ○ fascinating
   - ○ quotidian
   - ○ recalcitrant
   - ○ experimental
   - ○ amorphous

3. The (i)_____ clothing store faced its first real crisis just six months after opening when new owners took over the building, raised the rent (ii)_____, and asked for a five-year extension on the lease.

Blank (i)	Blank (ii)
fledgling	beneficently
urbane	precipitously
ostentatious	minutely

4. Ronald Reagan became known as "The Great Communicator" particularly because of his ability to make (i)_____ topics in domestic and foreign affairs more (ii)_____ to persons of widely varying educational levels.

Blank (i)	Blank (ii)
abstruse	palatable
obtuse	lucid
mundane	munificent

5. The census taker's (i)_____ job is made even
more difficult by the (ii)_____ nature of modern
civilization. Increasing numbers of people seldom reside
in any one place for very long. Even among those who
do remain (iii)_____, however, there are frequent
changes of livelihood, income, and even socioeconomic status.

Blank (i)	Blank (ii)	Blank (iii)
arduous	inert	itinerant
facile	transient	contrite
facetious	aesthetic	static

6. By nightfall the city council debate had long since
degenerated into (i)_____. What had begun in
the late afternoon as an earnest but polite discussion
turned personal as both sides hurled (ii)_____
and personal attacks at each other. Disinterested observers,
however, blamed the (iii)_____ chairman of the
council for allowing such disarray, arguing that a moderator
with more experience could have managed the meeting
more constructively.

Blank (i)	Blank (ii)	Blank (iii)
complacency	acclamations	neophyte
parity	perturbations	assiduous
bedlam	epithets	exuberant

Questions 7–9 refer to the following passage.

One popular but controversial way of regaining revenue shortfalls in professional sports is to sell stadium naming rights. Building a new sports or entertainment facility is a major financial undertaking; as branding and sponsorship become increasingly ubiquitous, it is perhaps inevitable that big business will shoulder more of the burden in exchange for publicity.

Theoretically, the selling of naming rights seems like a win-win proposition, but practically, the situation is more complicated. Fans are often opposed to changing the name of a stadium, or want to make sure their contribution to its construction is recognized. Neighborhood residents may also object to a perceived redecoration of their community in corporate colors, logos, and advertisements. For companies, naming rights alone often do not justify the high prices charged. Additionally, it is unclear whether the team or the facility benefits from the sale: if the corporation is a "sponsor," the team should receive the money, but facility owners glean revenue from "advertisers." Thus, the difficulty of reaching a mutually acceptable wording of complicated agreements creates a quagmire of litigation.

Several means of compromise have been negotiated, such as selling the name of the field while keeping the original name of the sports arena, selling sections of the facility, allowing a company to "present" it, allowing the sponsor to provide retail or concession services inside the stadium, and offering business opportunities such as direct-to-consumer coupons, product samples, and information. Though the practice was nearly unheard of thirty-five years ago, there are currently 72 sponsorship deals in place. And sports is not the only area to "go corporate"—convention centers, concert venues, public works, and even educational institutions have sold naming rights in exchange for much-needed funds and services.

7. The passage mentions the difference between "sponsors" and "advertisers" primarily in order to

○ illustrate the confusing nature of legal proceedings that surround naming rights' deals

○ provide an example of the kinds of issues that surround a naming rights agreement

○ prove that it is always important to consider terminology carefully

○ reveal the pernicious nature of one and the benevolent nature of the other

○ explain why communities often do not benefit from neighborhood stadiums

8. In which sentence of the passage does the author attempt to anticipate and preclude a possible reaction on the part of the reader?

○ Building a new sports or entertainment facility is a major financial undertaking; as branding and sponsorship become increasingly ubiquitous, it is perhaps inevitable that big business will shoulder more of the burden in exchange for publicity.

○ Theoretically, the selling of naming rights seems like a win-win proposition, but practically, the situation is more complicated.

○ For companies, naming rights alone often do not justify the high prices charged.

○ Thus, the difficulty of reaching a mutually acceptable wording of complicated agreements creates a quagmire of litigation.

○ Though the practice was nearly unheard of thirty-five years ago, there are currently 72 sponsorship deals in place.

9. In the context in which it appears in the last paragraph, the word "practice" most nearly means

○ observance

○ rite

○ rehearsal

○ action

○ office

Questions 10–11 refer to the following passage.

Often lost in the uproariously ribald nature of Aristophanes' great wartime comedy *Lysistrata* (411 BCE) is the author's serious message. Contemporary audiences, like modern ones, were taken by the story of Lysistrata organizing the Greek women to withhold sexual favors until peace is declared between Athens and Sparta. To its Athenian audience, though, embroiled in seemingly endless Peloponnesian War, the work had a clear symbolic meaning: end the war, but through celebration of Greek unity, not celibacy. The part meant to resonate with viewers was not the withholding of sex, but the power of the concord the women showed in so doing. The play's women, in fact, represent the Greek poleis, or city-states. The protagonists, Lysistrata and Lampito, represent Athens and Sparta, respectively; the conspiracy can't begin until Lampito arrives, and peace can be achieved only when they make common cause with the other women. The women's cohesion carries them through their confrontation with the magistrate and his henchmen, and is emphasized in the oracle: the ills of life will end when "the swallows...shall have all flocked together." And the men only finally agree to give the women a hearing when they realize that they're facing "a general conspiracy embracing all Greece." The men, for their part, represent anti-Greek, polis-based attitudes, and are only overcome when led by Lysistrata to focus on Greek commonalities, instances of past mutual aid, and the shared external threat of the Persians.

10. With which of the following statements would the author most likely agree?

   ○ Aristophanes was uniquely influential among Athenian playwrights.

   ○ Wartime comedies without a serious message are inappropriate subjects of study.

   ○ Some knowledge of history can be useful in interpreting literature from other eras.

11. The author mentions the oracle primarily in order to

   ○ emphasize the importance of Lampito among the conspirators

   ○ provide additional evidence in support of the main idea of the passage

   ○ clarify the origins of the conspiracy in the play

   ○ suggest that earlier interpretations of *Lysistrata* were based on false assumptions

   ○ concede a point in opposition to the main idea of the passage

Question 12 refers to the following passage.

Statistics released by the National Institute of Health show that cancer patients, on average, are living almost six months longer after the initial diagnosis of their condition than were patients just two years ago. Moreover, these findings conform to a trend that goes back well over a decade. Clearly, the medical community is making significant progress in extending the lives of cancer patients.

12. The above argument depends on which of the following as an assumption?

○ Cancer is not being diagnosed in progressively earlier stages.

○ The trend is more pronounced in some kinds of cancer than in others.

○ Fewer people are diagnosed with cancer each year.

○ The number of patients whose cancer goes into full remission is also rising.

○ Cancer is no longer the leading cause of death among people over 60 years of age.

13. Fervent schisms among the delegates were largely overplayed; the area of _____ was sizable enough to keep the convention from being disbanded.

☐ congruence

☐ asperity

☐ contradiction

☐ concurrence

☐ impassivity

☐ truculence

14. What Andrew Johnson lacked in education he made up for with his _____; though he never attended school, he taught himself to read and write, entered politics, and ultimately succeeded Abraham Lincoln as president of the United States.

☐ mettle

☐ timidity

☐ tenacity

☐ tenuousness

☐ candor

☐ alacrity

15. The _____ sales clerk, desperate to unload her burgeoning inventory, unwittingly drove many a potential customer away with her pushy, overeager manner.

☐ loquacious

☐ irreverent

☐ officious

☐ innocuous

☐ meddlesome

☐ vigilant

16. _____ is no guarantee of worker loyalty; even the most compliant of employees may be motivated by a hidden agenda.

☐ Effrontery

☐ Deference

☐ Prevarication

☐ Complaisance

☐ Truculence

☐ Chicanery

Questions 17–18 refer to the following passage.

Research conducted on the neurological consequences of
illicit substances traditionally has centered on the blockage of
the reuptake neurons (DAT) that, under normal conditions,
recycle dopamine (DA) to prevent overstimulation. As seen in
the brain of a healthy, non substance-abusing individual, DA
is released through an electric pulse, it lingers momentarily
around dopamine receptors (D2) to pique the body, and then
travels back up DAT for later use. Recently, positron emission
tomography has enabled researchers to a discover an unexpected, completely different process: drug use may actually
decrease the quantity of D2 available to receive DA, resulting
in a perceived deficit of the latter and an irrepressible compul-
sion, the hallmark of addiction, to increase its production
through stimulants.

17. In the context in which is appears, "pique" most nearly
    means

    ○ impair
    ○ heal
    ○ excite
    ○ relax
    ○ irritate

18. The passage explains the conventional focus of substance abuse research in order to

○ argue that such an approach is based on a false understanding of the way that most illegal drugs act on the brain

○ suggest that the positron emission technology is not accurate in its depiction of D2 reduction

○ provide evidence in favor of continuing research into DAT blockage

○ make clear why the discovery of an alternate consequence of substance abuse might be unexpected

○ offer a reasonable explanation for the inability of many people to overcome drug addiction

Questions 19–20 refer to the following passage.

One of the most significant reasons for the dramatic rise in both agricultural production and population in western Europe around 1000 CE was the increase in the use of horses as draft animals. The military preeminence of mounted cavalry since the Carolingian era meant that horses were selectively bred for size and strength earlier than were other farm animals, and the ninth-century development of nailed horseshoes improved both traction and resistance against infection. Most importantly, perhaps, harnesses designed for oxen were adapted for horses: a neck strap that restricted both air and blood from reaching the horse's brain was reconfigured to put the weight on the horse's shoulders, and horses quickly shed their ancient stigma as lazy beasts.

The change from ox to horse as the primary draft animal was slow and erratic. **Horses were expensive, untraditional, and required an expensive food, oats.** Where the change occurred, though, it gave the European countryside a new look by greatly increasing the amount of land that could be exploited from a central homestead. Where once farmers were limited to fields to which they could drive their oxen, plow, and return home in a day, they could now ride their horses much greater distances, do a day's work, and still return to safety before dark. Isolated hamlets grew towards each other to form vast villages, which, in turn, expanded into towns, and the great primeval forests of Europe receded into memory.

19. The passage provides information to answer which of the
    following questions?

    ○ How far from a central homestead could oxen be
      driven for a day's work?

    ○ What developments helped lead to the military
      primacy of horses?

    ○ What made ancient harnesses unsuitable for
      horses?

20. In the passage, the text in boldface plays which of the
    following roles?

    ○ It cites factors facilitating the development under
      discussion.

    ○ It cites factors inhibiting the development under
      discussion.

    ○ It eliminates an alternate cause for the
      development under discussion.

    ○ It resolves a paradox presented in the passage.

    ○ It suggests further ramifications of a paradox
      presented in the passage.

Math Drill 1

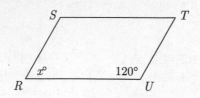

$RSTU$ is a parallelogram.

1.
Quantity A	Quantity B
x	45

○ Quantity A is greater.

○ Quantity B is greater.

○ The two quantities are equal.

○ The relationship cannot be determined from the information given.

2. Mr. Jones purchased a new bedroom set by using an extended payment plan. The regular price of the set was $900, but on the payment plan he paid $300 up front and 9 monthly payments of $69 each.

Quantity A

$23

Quantity B

The amount Mr. Jones paid in addition to the regular price of the bedroom set.

○ Quantity A is greater.

○ Quantity B is greater.

○ The two quantities are equal.

○ The relationship cannot be determined from the information given.

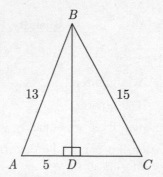

3.   **Quantity A**   **Quantity B**

The perimeter of   42
$\triangle BCD$

⟡ Quantity A is greater.

⟡ Quantity B is greater.

⟡ The two quantities are equal.

⟡ The relationship cannot be determined from the information given.

4. The circumference of a circle with a radius of $\frac{2}{5}$ meter is C meters.

    Quantity A   **Quantity B**
       C 4

⟡ Quantity A is greater.

⟡ Quantity B is greater.

⟡ The two quantities are equal.

⟡ The relationship cannot be determined from the information given.

5. **Quantity A**   **Quantity B**

    $x + 1$ $1 - x$

○ Quantity A is greater.

○ Quantity B is greater.

○ The two quantities are equal.

○ The relationship cannot be determined
  from the information given.

6. The average (arithmetic mean) of two positive integers is
   equal to 17. Each of the integers is greater than 12.

   Quantity A   **Quantity B**

   Twice the larger of   44
   the two integers

○ Quantity A is greater.

○ Quantity B is greater.

○ The two quantities are equal.

○ The relationship cannot be determined
  from the information given.

7. **Quantity A**   **Quantity B**

   xy $x\sqrt{y}$

○ Quantity A is greater.

○ Quantity B is greater.

○ The two quantities are equal.

○ The relationship cannot be determined from the information given.

8. **Quantity A**   **Quantity B**

   30   The number of integers from 15 to –15, inclusive

○ Quantity A is greater.

○ Quantity B is greater.

○ The two quantities are equal.

○ The relationship cannot be determined from the information given.

9. Mike bought a used car and had it repainted. If the cost of the paint job was one-fifth of the purchase price of the car, and if the cost of the car and the paint job combined was $4,800, then what was the purchase price of the car?

  ○ $800
  ○ $960
  ○ $3,840
  ○ $4,000
  ○ $4,250

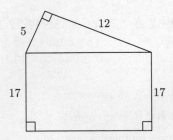

10. What is the perimeter of the figure above?

  ○ 51
  ○ 64
  ○ 68
  ○ 77
  ○ 91

11. If x and y are integers and xy is an even integer, which of the following must be an odd integer?

○ $xy + 5$

○ $x + y$

○ $\dfrac{x}{y}$

○ $4x$

○ $7xy$

12. If $3x = -2$, then $(3x - 3)^2 =$

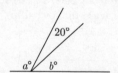

13. In the figure above, what does b equal if $a = 3b$?

○ 40

○ 30

○ 25

○ 20

○ 10

Questions 14–16 refer to the following chart.

REGISTERED VOTERS IN TOWNSHIP X IN 2010

Distribution by Age and Gender			Percent of Registered Voters by Political Affiliation	
Age	Male	Female	Affiliation	Percent
18 to 32	1,030	1,104	Democrat	43%
33 to 47	1,114	1,259	Republican	41%
48 to 62	1,291	1,306	Other, including Independent	16%
63+	947	1,002		
Total	4,382	4,671		

14. If the total number of registered voters in Township X increased 10% from 2000 to 2010, then how many registered voters were in Township X in 2000 ?

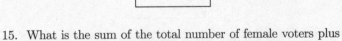

15. What is the sum of the total number of female voters plus the total number of remaining voters less than 48 years old in Township X in 2010 ?

- ○ 5,701
- ○ 5,715
- ○ 6,745
- ○ 6,815
- ○ 8,106

Crash Course for the GRE

16. In Township X in 2010, the ratio of the number of voters registered as Democrats to the number of male registered voters age 48 to 62 was most nearly

○ 1 to 1

○ 2 to 1

○ 3 to 1

○ 3 to 2

○ 5 to 2

17. What is the least number r for which $(3r + 2)(r - 3) = 0$?

○ -3

○ -2

○ $-\dfrac{2}{3}$

○ $\dfrac{2}{3}$

○ 3

18. What is the perimeter, in centimeters, of a rectangular newspaper ad 14 centimeters wide that has the same area as a rectangular newspaper ad 52 centimeters long and 28 centimeters wide?

$$\boxed{}$$

19. In a certain election, 60 percent of the voters were women. If 30 percent of the women and 20 percent of the men voted for candidate X, what percent of men and women voters in the election voted for candidate X ?

○ 18%

○ 25%

○ 26%

○ 30%

○ 50%

20. If $K = 21 \times 54 \times 22$, then which of the following is an integer?

Indicate all such integers.

☐ $\dfrac{K}{15}$

☐ $\dfrac{K}{27}$

☐ $\dfrac{K}{33}$

☐ $\dfrac{K}{48}$

☐ $\dfrac{K}{63}$

☐ $\dfrac{K}{75}$

Math Drill 2

1.   **Quantity A**   **Quantity B**
         $4(2^6)$ $6(4^2)$

   ○ Quantity A is greater.

   ○ Quantity B is greater.

   ○ The two quantities are equal.

   ○ The relationship cannot be determined
      from the information given.

2.   **Quantity A**   **Quantity B**

   The percent increase   The percent decrease
   from 4 to 5   from 5 to 4

   ○ Quantity A is greater.

   ○ Quantity B is greater.

   ○ The two quantities are equal.

   ○ The relationship cannot be determined from
      the information given.

3.   **Quantity A**   **Quantity B**

The circumference of a circular region with radius r The perimeter of a square with side r

○ Quantity A is greater.

○ Quantity B is greater.

○ The two quantities are equal.

○ The relationship cannot be determined from the information given.

4.

        Quantity A   **Quantity B**

The average (arithmetic mean) of 7, 3, 4, and 2   The average of $2a + 5$, $4a$, and $7 - 6a$

○ Quantity A is greater.

○ Quantity B is greater.

○ The two quantities are equal.

○ The relationship cannot be determined from the information given.

5. In the xy-plane, one of the vertices of square Q is the point $(-3, -4)$. The diagonals of Q intersect at the point $(2, 1)$.

Quantity A	Quantity B
The area of Q	100

○ Quantity A is greater.

○ Quantity B is greater.

○ The two quantities are equal.

○ The relationship cannot be determined from the information given.

6.

Quantity A	Quantity B
$3^{17} + 3^{18}$	$(4)3^{17}$

○ Quantity A is greater.

○ Quantity B is greater.

○ The two quantities are equal.

○ The relationship cannot be determined from the information given.

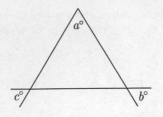

7.   **Quantity A**   **Quantity B**

         $b + c$ $180 - a$

○ Quantity A is greater.

○ Quantity B is greater.

○ The two quantities are equal.

○ The relationship cannot be determined
from the information given.

8. If the cost of a one-hour telephone call is $7.20, what
would be the cost of a ten-minute telephone call at the
same rate?

○ $7.10

○ $3.60

○ $1.80

○ $1.20

○ $0.72

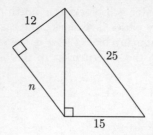

9. What is the value of n in the figure above?

○ 9
○ 15
○ 16
○ $12\sqrt{3}$
○ 20

10. If $x + y = z$ and $x = y$, then which of the following must be true?

Indicate <u>all</u> such equations.

☐ $2x + 2y = 2z$

☐ $x - y = 0$

☐ $x - z = y - z$

☐ $x = \dfrac{z}{2}$

☐ $x - y = 2z$

11. A movie theater is 3 blocks due north of a supermarket and a beauty parlor is 4 blocks due east of the movie theater. How many blocks long is the street that runs directly from the supermarket to the beauty parlor?

○ 2.5

○ 3

○ 4

○ 5

○ 7

12. The units digit of a 2-digit number is 3 times the tens digit. If the digits are reversed, the resulting number is 36 more than the original number. What is the original number?

○ 13

○ 26

○ 36

○ 62

○ 93

13. A restaurant owner sold 2 dishes to each of his customers at $4 per dish. At the end of the day, he had taken in $180, which included $20 in tips. How many customers did he serve?

┌─────────────┐
│   │
│   │
└─────────────┘

Questions 14–16 refer to the following graph.

PRIVATE DONATIONS TO CHARITABLE
CAUSES IN COUNTRY *X.* JAN. 1971–DEC. 1989

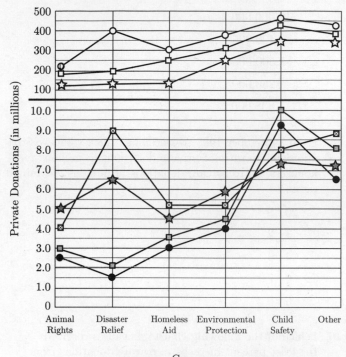

Cause

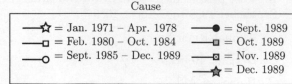

14. If there were 38 child safety organizations and the funds contributed to these organizations in September 1989 were evenly distributed, how much did each charity receive?

   ○ $12,000,000

   ○ $9,400,000

   ○ $2,500,000

   ○ $250,000

   ○ $38,000

15. From September 1985 to December 1989, what was the approximate ratio of private donations in millions for homeless aid to private donations in millions for animal rights?

   ○ 20 : 9

   ○ 3 : 2

   ○ 4 : 3

   ○ 9 : 7

   ○ 6 : 5

16. Which of the following charitable causes received the least percent increase in private donations from September 1989 to October 1989 ?

   ○ Animal Rights

   ○ Disaster Relief

   ○ Homeless Aid

   ○ Environmental Protection

   ○ Child Safety

17. Alex gave Jonathan a dollars. She gave Gina two dollars more than she gave Jonathan and she gave Louanne three dollars less than she gave Gina. In terms of a, how many dollars did Alex give Gina, Jonathan, and Louanne altogether?

○ $\dfrac{a}{3}$

○ $a - 1$

○ $3a$

○ $3a - 1$

○ $3a + 1$

18. If $m + n = p$, then $m^2 + 2mn + n^2 =$

○ $4p$

○ $np - m$

○ p^2

○ $p^2 + 4(m + p)$

○ $p^2 + np + m^2$

19. For all real numbers x and y, if $x * y = x(x - y)$,
    then $x * (x * y) =$

    ○ $x^2 - xy$

    ○ $x^2 - 2xy$

    ○ $x^3 - x^2 - xy$

    ○ $x^3 - (xy)^2$

    ○ $x^2 - x^3 + x^2y$

20. If x is an integer such that $1 < x < 10$, then which of
    the following could be the remainder when 117 is divided
    by x ?

    Indicate <u>all</u> such numbers.

    ☐ 1

    ☐ 2

    ☐ 3

    ☐ 4

    ☐ 5

    ☐ 6

    ☐ 7

PART IV

Drill Answers and Explanations

Verbal Drill 1

1. **D** The clue in the sentence is "Children...have become 'hasty viewers.'" The transition punctuation is a "same-direction" semicolon. So a good word for the blank would be wanders. In any case, it has to be a negative word. The words in (A), (B), and (E) are positive, and (C) isn't really negative. That leaves (D).

2. **C** Find the story. This architect doesn't promote himself; therefore, his fame can't be a result of self-promotion. Try a word like *fame* for the blank. Neither *proficiency* nor *temperament* mean "fame," so cross off (A) and (B). *Prominence* could work, so give (C) a "maybe" and move on. There is nothing in the sentence to indicate that the architect is superior, so eliminate (D). While the architect may have been reticent, you are looking for *fame*. Cross off (E). The best answer is (C).

3. **virtuosic, mellifluous**

    The clue "roused the audience to a standing ovation" indicates that both blanks need a positive word. The toughest part about filling either blank is the difficult vocab in the two columns. Use positive/negative to eliminate unlikely choices. *Hackneyed* sounds negative, while *virtuosic* looks a lot like *virtue*, a positive word. In the second column, *mellifluous* looks a bit like *mellow*, which is usually a good thing, but *insipid* has the prefix *in*, which means "against." That may give it a negative connotation. All told, *virtuosic* and *mellifluous* both have positive meanings and suit the sentence best.

4. **ambiguous, dissuade**

    The clue for the first blank, "such unproven programs," comes at the end of the sentence. You need a word meaning "inconclusive" to describe the results. *Conclusive* is clearly the opposite of what you want, but *ambiguous* looks good, especially given its prefix *ambi*, which means "going in both directions." *Auspicious*, in contrast, may sound like *suspicious*, but if you've been studying your vocabulary, you'll know that it has a positive meaning. Hang on to *ambiguous* and work the second blank. You already know that the program's results have not been proven, but the reverse-direction transition "however" indicates that those findings are having an unexpected or contradictory effect on parents' desire to enroll their children. Since the phrase "have failed to" comes right before the blank, you need a word meaning "discourage." Keep *disabuse* and *dissuade* if you're not sure of their meanings, but get rid of *distinguish*. Meanwhile, notice that *dissuade* shares the same word root as *persuade*, but has the prefix *dis*, which means "not." That makes it a likely choice, leaving *ambiguous* and *dissuade* as the two best answers.

5. **bliss, irrational, scant**

The reverse-direction transition "nonetheless" tells you that the first blank needs a word meaning the opposite of either "rational" or "pragmatic." Since there's no synonym for *irrational* in the first column, try "not practical" and use POE. While an impractical person might make his own suffering a priority—via *melancholy* or *discord*—*bliss* makes more sense, especially given that "regard for their own happiness" is mentioned later in the sentence. Another reverse-direction transition, "in contrast," is also used to reverse either "rational" or "pragmatic" for the second blank. Choose *irrational* from the second column and work on the third blank. The first part of the sentence tells you that classical economics sees humans as trying to maximize their own happiness, and then the reverse-direction transition "in contrast" gives you Veblen's view. As such, the third blank needs a word that means the opposite of "maximizing happiness." *Scant* is the closest match from the third column, making it, *bliss*, and *irrational* the best answers.

6. **plagiarism, proliferate, ensure**

The clue at the end of the sentence, "copying from a website," gives you *plagiarism* for the first blank. Use the second part of the sentence and the reverse transition "However" for the second blank; since their fears were not realized, you know you need a word like *increase*. If you don't know the word *proliferate*, studying your Greek roots can make it a great bet. For the last blank, you know that the educators are checking their students' work, so a good word for the last blank would be *prove*. *Rebut* is tempting but doesn't quite fit, and *neglect* isn't even close, so you're left with *ensure*, the correct answer.

7. **E** The conclusion of the argument is the first sentence—medieval stoneworkers are more skilled than modern ones—and the results of the survey provide the premise on which this conclusion is based. The argument assumes, though, that cathedrals are typical of medieval stonework; if not, the medieval masons are being evaluated on an atypical sample of their work. Thus, (E) most weakens the argument: If lower quality stonework is more likely to be destroyed, then medieval masons are being judged on their best work—their worst work likely having been destroyed long ago. Choices (A) and (B) would both strengthen the argument: (A), by removing a possible distinction between medieval and modern masons that might otherwise account for the difference in quality; (B), by directly supporting the above assumption. Without further information relating building size or apprenticeship length to skill in stonework, finally, both (C) and (D) are beyond the scope of the argument.

8. **C**   This is a main idea question about the passage as a whole. Your "treasure hunt" should have revealed that the passage is basically discussing the way in which Strachey interprets the English women's movement. Eliminate (B) right away because it's not about a "literary" work. Eliminate (D) because it's not a "novel analysis." Eliminate (A) and (E) because they are too specific. That leaves (C).

9. **C**   For line reference questions, go back to the lines cited, and read about five lines before and after those lines. You can find the answer in either place for this question. The first sentence of the paragraph tells you Strachey is writing about "the historical connections between the women's movement and other social and political developments." Choice (C) is just a paraphrase of this.

10. **B**   Look back in the passage for the place where the author "faults" Strachey. It's in the last paragraph. The author states, "Where Strachey pictured a relatively fixed image of domestic women throughout the first half of the 19th century, recent historical and literary works suggest that this image was both complex and unstable." Sounds like (B).

11. **D**   First, go back to the passage to find out what the author said about "the similarity between the English and American women's movements." It's at the end of the first paragraph. The author says that "like its American counterpart, the English women's movement had a powerful sense of its own historic importance and of its relationship to wider social and political change." So you're looking for an answer choice that would indicate that was not true. Choice (D) directly contradicts the author's assertion.

12. unrecognizable, reworked

The best word for the blank here is something like "new" since you know that it is very different and you have the change-direction transition "Though." The best two answers, therefore, are *unrecognizable* and *reworked*. None of the other choices really match each other or the meaning of the blank.

13. furtive, surreptitious

The clue for the blank is "he had ulterior motives." Think "sneaky" or "secretive" and use POE. *Inconspicuous* is out, since it's the opposite of the clue, but hang onto *furtive* (even if you don't know its meaning). *Overt* is also the opposite of sneaky; get rid of it. *Unorthodox* and *predictable*, meanwhile, don't match the clue, but *surreptitious* does. That leaves *furtive* and *surreptitious*, the two best answers.

14. urbane, cosmopolitan

Since the hotel had both "refined interiors" and an "amply stocked reading room," it would appeal to guests who were well-read and liked refinement. Think "sophisticated" or "worldly" and use POE. *Philistine* is the opposite of refined or worldly, but both *urbane* and *cosmopolitan* are solid matches. In contrast, *uncouth*'s meaning is very similar to that of *philistine*, so cross out that choice. *Grandiloquent* and *pretentious*, meanwhile, don't match the clue, leaving you with *urbane* and *cosmopolitan*.

15. amiable, affable

"His inherent irascibility" is reversed by the change-direction transition "not," which comes before the blank describing Wilbert. You need a word that means the opposite of *irascibility*. Think "friendly" or "good-tempered" and use POE. Neither *loquacious* nor *pedantic* means friendly, but *amiable* matches. *Garrulous*, meanwhile, has the same meaning as *loquacious*, so cross it out. Finally, *affable* is a good match, but *stentorian* doesn't work. *Amiable* and *affable* suit the sentence best.

16.   **It is hard from our modern perspective to imagine that theater has the power to influence politics, yet the plays of pre-republican Ireland did just that.**

The passage starts out with its conclusion that, in the case of Ireland, theater influenced politics. The rest of the paragraph tells how this occurred.

17. C   Go back to the first paragraph. In lines 6–7 the passage states, "In some localities the mosquito was abundant but malaria rare or absent."

18. C   Try putting your own word in the passage to replace "host." The transition "but" indicates that the reference to distinct biological traits should contrast with the statement that the mosquitoes seem almost identical, so you need a word that means something like "large number." Of the choices, *multitude* is the best match. Beware of (A), which, though tempting, refers specifically to people. Likewise, be careful with (E): While the mosquitoes in question do, in fact, support parasites, that usage wouldn't make sense in this context.

19. A   Reread the second sentence of the second paragraph. It says that the mosquito becomes a carrier when it feeds on human blood.

20. **E**   Choice (E) is best supported in the passage. The first paragraph discusses a seemingly inconsistent relationship between the presence of the mosquitoes and the prevalence of malaria, a paradox resolved by the discovery of multiple species among the insects; the boldface text suggests why this multiplicity of species wasn't immediately apparent. Choices (C) and (D), while appropriately referring to the paradox, incorrectly describe the value of the bolded text: It neither resolves nor clarifies the importance of that paradox. Choices (A) and (B), finally, are not supported because the boldface text doesn't directly weaken or strengthen the author's main point, which is the discussion of one important step in the effort to eradicate malaria.

     Crash Course for the GRE

Verbal Drill 2

1. **C**   That semicolon is transition punctuation. It tells you that the first part of the sentence agrees with the second part. The second part contains the clue "what one group sees as peacekeeping, another group might see as subjugation." How can you describe that—it sounds like a contradiction. How about "contradictory" for the blank? Time to go to the answers. You can eliminate (A), *academic*, because it doesn't mean "contradictory." Choice (B), *portentous*, means "predicting the future," which might be true of historical events but has nothing to do with this sentence. Choice (C), *paradoxical*, means "seemingly contradictory," so keep it. (If you weren't sure, you'd keep it in anyway.) Choice (D), *trifling*, means "frivolous" or "of little value," so eliminate it. Choice (E), *bellicose*, which might be true of some historical events but has nothing to do with this sentence. The best answer is (C).

2. **B**   The clue for the blank after the transition word "however" is "daily routines," so the word in the blank can be "routine." That definitely eliminates (A), (D), and (E). If you know what *quotidian* or *recalcitrant* means, you know the answer is (B). If you don't, (C) is a good guess (although it's wrong).

3. **fledgling, precipitously**

   The only thing that we really know about the store is that it is pretty new, so "new" would be a good word for the first blank. While *urbane* and *ostentatious* could both apply to a clothing store, they do not match the meaning of the clue. Since you know that the situation is a crisis, a good word for the second blank would be something like "a lot." The best answer, then, is *precipitously*, since none of the other choices match the direction of the clue.

4. **abstruse, lucid**

What would earn Reagan the distinction of "The Great Communicator," other than an ability to make difficult or complicated topics easy to understand? Hang on to *abstruse*, but don't fall for the trap of *obtuse*. You can also cross out *mundane*, as it means "common" or "ordinary"—not "complicated." Moving to the second blank, think "clear" or "understandable," given the first part of the sentence. *Palatable* is close, but *lucid* is a much more precise match. *Munificent*, meanwhile, doesn't mean "understandable," making *abstruse* and *lucid* the best choices.

5. **arduous, transient, static**

"Is made even more difficult" is the clue for the first blank. Recycle "difficult" and use POE. Only *arduous* matches. Regarding the second blank, the clue "people seldom reside in any one place for very long" suggests a word meaning "moving around" or "mobile." *Inert* is the opposite of the clue, and *aesthetic* doesn't match, so choose *transient* and work the third blank. The change-direction transition "however," which comes right after the blank, calls for a word meaning the opposite of mobile. *Static* is a strong match, making it, *arduous*, and *transient* the best choices.

6. **bedlam, epithets, neophyte**

The second and third blanks might be a little easier on this one. A good word for the third blank would be something like "inexperienced," since you are told that a person with "more experience" would have handled things better. The best choice, then, is *neophyte*. For the second blank, a good word would be something like "insults," since you are told that things were getting personal. The best answer here is *epithets*. For the first blank a good word would be something like "chaos," since the meeting started out well but resulted in disarray. The best answer here is *bedlam*.

7. **B**   The point about how different terminology can determine who benefits is an example of an issue that makes selling naming rights legally complicated, which is (B). Naming rights may be complicated, but they are not described as "confusing" (A). Choice (C) draws too large a conclusion from a specific example. Choice (D) is too extreme for the situation described. The differences in benefits are between facility owners and teams; the terminology does not affect the community's benefits (E). Therefore, the best answer is (B).

8. **B**   In the credited response, the author suggests that the naming rights may seem like a win-win proposition. However, the rest of the sentence—and the rest of the paragraph—is devoted to enumerating some of the difficulties and concerns that such deals often raise.

9. **D**   Try putting your own word in the passage to replace "practice." The transition "Though" indicates that the first part of the sentence will contrast with the current proliferation of sponsorships, so a word that means "activity" or "deed" might make sense—anything that conveys the meaning that it was once unheard of for something to happen. Of the choices, *action* is the best fit.

10. **C**   Choice (A) is not supported, as the passage makes no mention of other playwrights to whom a comparison can be made. Choice (B) is also not supported: The focus here is on a wartime comedy with a serious message, but the author doesn't comment on the propriety of studying this or any other play. Choice (C) is supported

by the main idea of the passage—that *Lysistrata* has an oft-overlooked meaning that depends on the political situation in Greece at the time of its composition.

11. **B**   Choice (B) is best supported by the passage: The oracle is brought up in a list of examples supporting the importance of the idea of Greek unity in the play. Choices (A) and (C) can be eliminated because the passage doesn't directly relate the oracle to Lampito or the origin of the conspiracy. Choice (D) is also not supported: Although a superficial interpretation of *Lysistrata* is being questioned, the passage doesn't provide enough information to characterize either interpretation as earlier. Choice (E), finally, is backwards, as the oracle supports the author's emphasis on cohesion in the play.

12. **A**   The conclusion of the argument is at the end: "Significant progress is being made toward the extending the lives of cancer patients." The premise on which the argument is based is that patients are living longer after their initial diagnosis. For this argument to be valid, though, you need to assume that length of life is the same thing as time after initial diagnosis. Hence, (A) is the best response: If cancer is being diagnosed progressively earlier, then people could be aware of their condition longer without living any longer. Keep a close eye on the scope of the argument to help you eliminate the incorrect choices. The argument isn't about a comparison among types of cancer, or between cancer and other diseases, so eliminate (B) and (E). Likewise, the argument isn't about the number of either cancer diagnoses or people who make full recoveries, so eliminate (C) and (D).

13. **congruence, concurrence**

"Fervent schisms...were largely overplayed" is the clue indicating that the blank needs a word meaning the opposite of disagreement. Think "agreement" and use POE.

Congruence matches, but *asperity* and *contradiction* go in the opposite direction of agreement. *Concurrence*, like *congruence*, matches the clue, but *impassivity* and *truculence*, like the second and third choices, go in the opposite direction of the clue. That leaves *congruence* and *concurrence* as the two best answers.

14. mettle, tenacity

The blank needs a word meaning "perseverance" or "determination," given the semicolon, which acts as a same-direction transition, followed by the rest of the sentence, which discusses all that Johnson achieved "though he never attended school." *Mettle* works, but *timidity* does not. *Tenacity*, like *mettle*, is a good match for perseverance, but *tenuousness* goes in the opposite direction. Apply your clue word to the two remaining choices. Does *candor* mean perseverance? What about *alacrity*? Neither one matches, leaving you with *mettle* and *tenacity*, the two best answers.

15. officious, meddlesome

What does the sentence tell you about the sales clerk? From the clue "drove many a potential customer away with her pushy, overeager manner," you can recycle "pushy" or "overeager" for the blank and use POE. Eliminate *loquacious* and *irreverent* if you know what they mean (here's where knowing your vocab comes in handy). *Officious*, on the other hand, could work, but *innocuous* doesn't mean anything close to pushy, so cross it out. *Meddlesome*, like *officious*, matches the clue, but *vigilant* doesn't mean pushy or overeager. That leaves you with *officious* and *meddlesome*, which are the two best choices.

16. **complaisance, deference**

The clue for the blank is "even the most compliant of employees." Recycle part of the clue word and apply "compliancy" to the answer choices. *Effrontery* and *Truculence* go in the opposite direction of "compliancy," so toss those two. *Deference* makes sense (think *defer*), but cross out both *Prevarication* and *Chicanery*, since they have to do with dishonesty (don't let the phrase "motivated by a hidden agenda" shift your focus away from the clue for the blank, which describes compliant employees). *Complaisance*, in contrast, agrees with the clue, making it and *Deference* the two best choices.

17. **C**   The first sentence of the passage says that dopamine is recycled to prevent overstimulation. This clue tells you that released dopamine must have a stimulating effect, so *pique* means "stimulate." Neither (A) nor (D) has this meaning. Choice (E) specifies a negative stimulation, which is not supported by the text. Choice (B) is also not supported by context. *Excite* is a good synonym for "stimulate" and is the correct choice.

18. **D**   Choice (A) is not supported by the text because the discovery of a different process does not necessarily make the old one incorrect. The same logic applies when considering (B); that one method is traditional does not make a different one incorrect. The passage never gives any indication of preferences or personal beliefs, so (C) is also incorrect. Choice (E) goes too far in saying that many people cannot overcome addiction; the passage does not offer statistics on recovery. Choice (D) is correct because the first sentence indicates a long-standing belief in DAT blockage as the primary problem.

19. **C**   Choice (A) is not supported: The passage suggests that the manageable distance for oxen was less than that for horses, but no specifics are provided for either animal.

Choice (B) is also not supported, as the passage focuses on agricultural developments; the military preeminence of mounted cavalry is only mentioned as inspiring early selective breeding. Choice (C), finally, is supported by the passage: The first paragraph indicates that the neck strap of the older harnesses inhibited the flow of both air and blood to the horse's brain.

20. **B** Choice (B) is best supported: The passage discusses the move to horses as primary draft animals, and the boldface text gives factors that hindered that transition. Choices (A) and (C), then, both contradict the passage and can be eliminated. Choices (D) and (E) are also not supported by the passage. Although the factors in bold-face might be considered part of a paradox—how horses overtook oxen despite significant disadvantages—the information presented neither solves nor further explores the ramifications of any such paradox.

Math Drill 1

1. **A**   In a parallelogram, opposite angles are equal, and the big angle plus the small angle adds up to 180°. So $x + 120 = 180$. That makes the value of Quantity A 60, which is greater than the 45 in Quantity B. The correct answer is (A).

2. **A**   To find the amount Mr. Jones paid in addition to the regular price of the bedroom set, multiply $69 by 9 months to get $621. Then add the $300 payment. $621 + 300 = 921$. So Mr. Jones paid an additional $21. The $23 in Quantity A is greater than the $21 in Quantity B. The correct answer is (A).

3. **B**   To find the perimeter of triangle *BCD,* find the length of *BD.* First, recognize the common Pythagorean triple 5-12-13. Therefore, *BD* = 12. Now find the third side of triangle *BCD.* Recognize that triangle *BCD* is a 9-12-15 multiple of the Pythagorean triple 3-4-5. So *DC* is 9. Next, add up the sides of triangle *BCD,* to find the perimeter: $9 + 12 + 15 = 36$. Quantity A is 36. Because Quantity B is 42, the correct answer is (B).

4. **B**   The formula for circumference is $C = 2\pi r$. Because $r = \frac{2}{5}$, $\left(C = 2\pi\left(\frac{2}{5}\right)\right)$, or $\frac{4}{5}\pi$. Quantity A is $\frac{4}{5}\pi$. Remember that π is about 3, so Quantity A is about $\frac{12}{5}$, which is a little more than 2. Quantity B is 4, which is greater. The correct answer is (B).

5. **D**   This is a Plugging In problem, so Plug In an easy number. Try $x = 2$. If $x = 2$, then Quantity A is 3 and Quantity B is −1, so eliminate (B) and (C). Now Plug In again

using one of the FROZEN numbers. Try $x = 0$. Quantity A is 1 and Quantity B is 1. Because the two quantities are equal, eliminate (A). The correct answer is (D).

6. **B** Because the question involves averages, draw an Average Pie. The average is 17, and the number of things is 2. Multiply the average by the number of things to find the total, which is 34. The two numbers have to add up to 34, but neither of them can be 12 or less. Because Quantity A is twice the greater of the two integers, find the greater integer by using the least integer allowed by the problem, which is 13. If the total is 34, and one number is 13, that means the other number is 21 because $21 + 13 = 34$. Quantity A is 42, which is twice 21. Quantity B is 44, so the correct answer is (B).

7. **D** First, Plug In easy numbers. Try $x = 3$ and $y = 4$; 4 is a good number to Plug In for y, because $\sqrt{4}$ is an integer. Therefore, Quantity A is 12 and Quantity B is 6. Quantity A is greater, so eliminate (B) and (C). Now Plug In again using FROZEN numbers. Try $x = 0$ and $y = 0$. Now Quantity A and Quantity B are both zero, making them equal, so eliminate (A). The correct answer is (D).

8. **B** First, there are no variables in this problem, so eliminate (D). The word "inclusive" in Quantity B means both -15 and 15 are included in the list of integers. Write out the list: $-15, -14, -13, -12, -11, -10, -9, -8, -7, -6, -5, -4, -3, -2, -1, 0, 1, 2, 3, 4, 5, 6, 7, 8, 9, 10, 11, 12, 13, 14, 15$. There are 31 integers. Because Quantity (A) is 30, Quantity B is greater. The correct answer is (B).

9. **D** The answer choices in this question represent information directly asked in the question, and the question can be solved by writing and solving an equation,

so use Plug In the Answers (PITA). Begin with (C). If the purchase price of the car is $3,840 and the cost of the paint job was one-fifth of the purchase price of the car, then the cost of the paint job is $\left(\frac{1}{5}\right)$$3,840 = $768. Therefore, the cost of the car and the paint job combined is $3,840 + $768 = $4,608. This is less than the combined cost identified by the question, so eliminate (C). Eliminate (A) and (B) as well, as they will result in a total cost that is even less than (C). Now, try (D). If the purchase price of the car is $4,000 and the cost of the paint job was one-fifth of the purchase price of the car, then the cost of the paint job is $\left(\frac{1}{5}\right)$$4,000 = $800. Therefore, the cost of the car and the paint job combined is $4,000 + $800 = $4,800. This matches the total identified by the question. The correct answer is (D).

10. **B**   To find the perimeter of the figure, the missing side of the rectangle needs to be identified. The missing side is the same length as the hypotenuse of the triangle. Solve for the hypotenuse. Either use the Pythagorean Theorem or recognize that the triangle is a 5-12-13 Pythagorean triple. Because the hypotenuse of the triangle is 13, the missing side is of the rectangle is 13. Now add up all the sides of the figure to get the perimeter: 5 + 12 + 17 + 13 + 17 = 64. The correct answer is (B).

11. **A**   Remember to Plug In more than once on "must be" problems. First, try $x = 2$ and $y = 3$. Choice (A) is $(2)(3) + 5 = 11$, which is odd so keep (A). Choice (B) is $2 + 3 = 5$, which is also odd so keep (B). Choice (C) is $\frac{2}{3}$, which is not an integer so eliminate (C). Choice (D) is $(4)(2) = 8$, which is even so eliminate (D). Choice (E) is $(7)(2)(3) = 42$, which is also even so eliminate (E). Now Plug In again using FROZEN numbers such as $x = 2$ and $y = 10$. Choice (A) is $(2)(10) + 5 = 25$, which is odd so keep (A). Choice (B) is $2 + 10 = 12$, which is even so eliminate (B). The correct answer is (A).

12. **25**   Substitute -2 for $3x$ in the problem to yield $(-2 - 3)^2$, or $(-5)^2$, which equals 25. The correct answer is 25.

13. **A**   A line has 180°, so $a + 20 + b = 180$, therefore $a + b = 160$. The problem also states that $a = 3b$. Now use PITA and Plug In the Answers for b, looking for the answer choice that produces values of a and b that sum to 160. Begin with (C). If $b = 25$, then $a = 75$. So $25 + 75 = 100$, which is less than 160. Therefore, eliminate (C). Eliminate (D) and (E) as well because they will produce lesser values. Try (A). If $b = 40$, then $a = 120$. So, $40 + 120 = 160$, which matches the target answer. Therefore, the correct answer is (A).

14. **8,230**   The problem states that the number of registered voters in Township X increased 10% from 2000 to 2010. In 2010, there were 4,382 male voters and 4,671 female voters for a total of 9,053 voters. The 9,053 voters in 2010 is 110% of the number of voters in 2000, so

translate that into the equation $9{,}053 = \frac{110}{100}x$. Solve for the value of x to find that the number of voters in 2000 was 8,230. The correct answer is 8,230.

15. **D**   The total number of females is 4,671. The question also asks for the total number of voters less than 48 years old. However, the females voters who are less than 48 years old have already been counted. Therefore, only add the number of male voters less than 48 years old, which is $1{,}030 + 1{,}114 = 2{,}144$. Therefore, the sum of the number of female voters and the number of remaining voters less than 48 years old is $4{,}671 + 2{,}144 = 6{,}815$. The correct answer is (D).

16. **C**   Find the ratio of the percentages of Democrats to the percentage of male voters age 48 to 62. The chart already provides the percentage of Democrats, so calculate the percentage of male voters age 48 to 62. To find out the percentage of male voters age 48 to 62, translate "1,291 is what percent of 9,053?" into $1{,}291 = \frac{x}{100}(9{,}053) = 14.2\%$. The ratio of 43% to 14% is closest to 3 to 1. The correct answer is (C).

17. **C**   The answer choices in this question represent the information directly asked for by the question, and the question could be solved by writing and solving an equation, so Plug In the Answers. Because the question is asking for the least number, start by Plugging In (A). Choice (A) is $\{3(-3) + 2\} \{-3 - 3\} = (-7)(-6) = 42$, which isn't

0. Eliminate (A). Choice (B) is $\{3(-2) + 2\}\{-2 - 3\} = (-4)(-5) = 20$, which isn't 0. Eliminate (B). Choice (C) is $\{3\left(-\frac{2}{3}\right) + 2\}\{-\frac{2}{3} - 3\} = (0)(-3\frac{2}{3}) = 0$. The correct answer is (C).

18. **236** The newspaper ad with a width of 14 has the same area as another ad 52 long and 28 wide, so calculate the area of the second ad using the formula $A = l \times w$: $52 \times 28 = 1{,}456$. Now use the area formula again to find the length of the first ad: $1456 = l \times 14$, so $l = 104$. In order to find the perimeter of the first ad, use the formula $P = 2l + 2w$: $P = 2(104) + 2(14) = 236$. The answer is 236.

19. **C** Because this question involves taking percentages of an unknown amount, this is a Hidden Plug In question. Plug In for the total number of voters. Make the total number of voters 100. 60% of the voters are women, so that's 60 women, and the remaining voters are men, so that's 40 men. 30% of the women voted for candidate X, so 30% of 60, which is $\frac{30}{100}(60)$, or 18 women, voted for candidate X. 20% of the men voted for candidate X, so 20% of 40, which is $\frac{20}{100}(40)$, or 8 men, voted for candidate X. Therefore, the total number of men and women voting for candidate X is $18 + 8$, or 26. 26 voters out of 100 total voters is 26%. The correct answer is (C).

20. **B, C,** and **E**

Factor 21, 54, and 22 into their prime factors: $21 = 7 \times 3$, $54 = 3 \times 3 \times 3 \times 2$, and $22 = 2 \times 11$, making a combined prime factorization of $2 \times 2 \times 3 \times 3 \times 3 \times 3 \times 7 \times 11$. In order for $21 \times 54 \times 22$ to be divisible by a number, all the factors of that number must also be factors of $21 \times 54 \times 22$. Find the prime factorization of all the denominators of the answer choices. The denominators in (A) and (F) each have 5 as a factor, which $21 \times 54 \times 22$ does not, so eliminate these answer choices. Choice (D) has too many 2's, so eliminate it as well. All the factors of the denominators in (B), (C), and (E) are also factors of $21 \times 54 \times 22$, and so these fractions will yield integers. The answer is (B), (C), and (E).

Math Drill 2

1. **A**   Because there are no variables in either Quantity A or Quantity B, eliminate (D). Now, find the prime factorization of Quantity A and Quantity B to compare their values. The prime factorization of Quantity A is $4(2^6) = 2^8$. The prime factorization of Quantity B is $6(4^2) = 2 \times 3 \times (2^2)^2 = 2 \times 3 \times 2^4 = 2^5 \times 3$. Both quantities contain at least 2^5, so compare the values by eliminating 2^5 from both quantities. Quantity A is now 2^3 and Quantity B is now 3. Because 2^3 is greater than 3, the correct answer is (A).

2. **A**   This is a Quant Comp question with only real numbers, so eliminate (D) as a values can be determined for both quantities. Use the formula for percent change, which is the difference divided by the original, multiplied by 100, to evaluate both quantities. In Quantity A, the difference is 1, and the original number is 4, so that's $\frac{1}{4}(100) = 25\%$. The percent change in Quantity A is 25%. In Quantity B, the difference is 1, and the original number is 5, so that's $\frac{1}{5}(100) = 20\%$. The percent change in Quantity B is 20%. Therefore, Quantity A is greater than Quantity B. The correct answer is (A).

3. **A**   This is a Quant Comp question with variables, so Plug In more than once. Begin with an easy number, such as $r = 2$. If $r = 2$, then Quantity A is $2\pi r = 4\pi$ and Quantity B is $4(2) = 8$. Because π is approximately 3, Quantity A is approximately 12. Therefore, Quantity A is greater than

Quantity B. Eliminate (B) and (C). Now Plug In again using FROZEN numbers. Plug In $r = \frac{1}{2}$. Then Quantity A is π and Quantity B is 2. Quantity A is greater again. Plugging In zero or a negative number is not allowed here because r is the radius of the circle and the side of the square. No matter what number is Plugged In for r, Quantity A is greater. The correct answer is (A).

4. **C**   Both quantities involve averages, so draw an Average Pie for both. In Quantity A, the total is $7 + 3 + 4 + 2 = 16$, and the number of things is 4, so the average, and Quantity A, is 4. Quantity B is the average of $2a + 5$, $4a$, and $7 - 6a$, so Plug In a number for a. Try $a = 2$. If $a = 2$, then the total in Quantity B is $9 + 8 - 5 = 12$, and the number of things is 3, so the average of Quantity B is 4. The two quantities are equal, so eliminate (A) and (B). Now Plug In again for Quantity B using FROZEN numbers. Try $a = 0$. If $a = 0$, then the total in Quantity B is $5 + 0 + 7$. The number of things is 3, so the average is still 4. $5 + 0 + 7 = 12$, which, when divided by the number of things, 3, gives an average of 4. In fact, no matter what number is used for a, the two quantities are always equal. The correct answer is (C).

5. **C**   There are no variables in this Quant Comp question, so eliminate (D). If one of the vertices of square Q is at $(-3, -4)$ and the point $(2, 1)$ is the midpoint of the square, then the vertex is 5 horizontal units and 5 vertical units away from the midpoint. This means that the distance between the midpoint and the vertex on the same diagonal as $(-3, -4)$ is also 5 right and 5 up from the midpoint. Therefore, the diagonal follows to the point $(7, 6)$, which is also a vertex of the square. Because it is a square, all the sides are equal length, so determine

the distance between x or y values of points $(-3, -4)$ and $(7, 6)$. The distance between the x values is 10, which means all the sides of square Q are 10. Quantity A asks for the area of square Q which is $10^2 = 100$. This is the same value as Quantity B, so the quantities are equal. The correct answer is (C).

6. **C**   Because there are no variables in either Quantity A or Quantity B, eliminate (D). Factor the expressions in both Quantity A and Quantity B. In Quantity A, factoring out 3^{17} results in $3^{17}(1 + 3^1)$, or $3^{17}(4)$. This is the same value as Quantity B. The correct answer is (C).

7. **C**   Plug In on geometry problems with variables. Plug In $a = 50$, and make the two angles inside the triangle opposite of angles b and c 60 and 70°, respectively. Any numbers will work as long as they add up to 180°, the number of degrees in a triangle. Because b and c are vertical angles to the 60- and 70-degree angles in the triangle, angle b is 60° and angle c is 70°. Now, evaluate the quantities. Quantity A is, $b + c = 60 + 70 = 130$. Quantity B is $180 - 50 = 130$. The two quantities are equal. The correct answer is (C).

8. **D**   The question states that a one-hour telephone call is $7.20. Use this information to figure out the price for a 10-minute telephone call by setting up a proportion. The proportion is $\frac{7.20}{60} = \frac{x}{10}$. Cross-multiply to find that $72.00 = 60(x)$. Divide by 60 to find that $x = \$1.20$. The correct answer is (D).

9. **C**   Manipulate the triangles to find the value of n. Begin with the triangle that has two known sides. Notice that this is a 15-20-25 multiple of the 3-4-5 Pythagorean triple. So the third side of this triangle is 20. Use this information to solve for n. Notice that this triangle is a

12-16-20 multiple of the 3-4-5 Pythagorean triple. So $n = 16$. The correct answer is (C).

10. **A, B, C,** and **D**

This is a "must be" problem, so Plug In more than once. Start with an easy number such as $x = 2$. If $x = 2$, then $y = 2$ and z equals 4. Now test the answer choices. For (A), $4 + 4 = 8$ which is true, so keep (A). For (B), $2 - 2 = 0$, which is also true, so keep (B). For (C), $2 - 4 = 2 - 4$, which is also true, so keep (C). For (D), $2 = \frac{4}{2}$, which is also true, so keep (D). For (E), $2 - 2 = 8$, which is not true, so eliminate (E). Now Plug In again using the FROZEN numbers such as $x = 10$. If $x = 10$, then $y = 10$, and $z = 20$. Test all of the remaining answer choices again. All the remaining choices are still true. In fact, no matter what numbers are used for the variables, (A), (B), (C), and (D) are all true. The correct answer is (A), (B), (C), and (D).

11. **D** Begin this problem by drawing the information given in the picture. The information in the question should form a 3:4:5 right triangle, so the street from the supermarket to the beauty parlor is 5 blocks long. The answer is (D).

12. **B** Plug In the Answers (PITA). The correct answer will meet the following criteria. The first condition is that the number's second digit must be 3 times the first digit. Choices (C), (D), and (E) all fail the first condition because the units digits are not three times the tens digits. Eliminate them. Now apply the second condition, that the reversed form of the number must be 36 more

than the original number, to the two remaining answer choices. For (A), 31 is not 36 more than 13, so eliminate (A). For (B), 62 is 36 more than 26. The correct answer is (B).

13. **20**   Solve this problem in bite-sized pieces. Start by subtracting the tips to get the total cost of the customers' dishes: $180 − $20 = $160. Now divide that by the total amount each customer spent to find the number of customers. If each customer bought two $4 dishes, then each customer spent $8 total, and $160 ÷ $8 = 20. The correct answer is 20.

14. **D**   Divide the $9.4 million in private donations received by child safety organizations in September 1989 by the 38 organizations operating at the time. The amount is approximately $250,000.The correct answer is (D).

15. **C**   From the line graph, you see that homeless aid groups took in about $300 million in private donations, and animal rights groups about $225 million. The ratio of $300 million to $225 million is 4 to 3. The correct answer is (C).

16. **E**   Identify the markers for September 1989 and October 1989 on the chart. The question is asking about the least percent increase between these two data points. So, begin by evaluating the data points. All of the differences between the data points for these two months are very similar; they all seem to have a difference of approximately 0.5. Because 0.5 is a lesser percent of a greater number, the least percent increase corresponds to the data point with the greatest numbers. Therefore, the correct answer is (E), child safety. Alternatively, find the percent increase for each of the answer choices by dividing the difference between the two points by the original, which in this case is the number for September

1989. The least percent increase is still (E), child safety, which is the correct answer.

17. **E**   There are variables in the question and answer choices, so this is a Plugging In problem. Plug In and work this problem in bite-sized pieces. Plug In a number for a such as $a = 10$. If Alex gave Jonathon 10 dollars, and she gave Gina two dollars more than she gave Jonathan, then she gave Gina 12 dollars. She gave Louanne three dollars less than she gave Gina, so she gave Louanne 9 dollars. So altogether, Alex gave Gina, Jonathan, and Louanne $10 + 12 + 9 = 31$ dollars, which is the target number. Plug In for the answer choices to find which one matches the target number. Choice (A) is $\frac{10}{3}$, which does not equal 31, so eliminate (A). Choice (B) is $10 - 1$, which does not equal 31, so eliminate (B). Choice (C) is $3(10)$, which does not equal 31, so eliminate (C). Choice (D) is $3(10) - 1$, which does not equal 31, so eliminate (D). Choice (E) is $3(10) + 1 = 31$. This matches the target number. The correct answer is (E).

18. **C**   The equation $m^2 + 2mn + n^2$ is just the common quadratic $x^2 + 2xy + y^2$, which can be rewritten as $(x + y)^2$, so rewrite $m^2 + 2mn + n^2$ as $(m + n)^2$. Because $m + n = p$, replace the $m + n$ in the $(m + n)^2$ with the p to get p^2. The correct answer is (C).

19. **E**   This is a function problem, so Plug In for the variables and follow the directions. Plug In $x = 2$ and $y = 3$. The problem states that $x * y = x(x - y)$ and asks for the value of $x * (x * y)$. Begin with the portion

inside the parentheses. $x * y = 2 * 3 = 2(2 - 3) = -2$. Now the question reads $x * -2$, which is the same as $2 * -2 = 2(2 - (-2)) = 2(2 + 2) = 8$, which is the target number. Plug In the values for x and y into the answer choices and look for one that matches the target answer. Choice (A) is $2^2 - 2(3) = -2$, which does not match the target number, so eliminate (A). Choice (B) is $2^2 - 2(2)(3) = -8$, which does not match the target number so eliminate (B). Choice (C) is $2^3 - 2^2 - 2(3) = 8 - 4 - 6 = -2$, which does not match the target number, so eliminate (C). Choice (D) is $2^3 - (2 \times 3)^2 = 8 - 36 = -28$, which does not match the target number, so eliminate (D). Choice (E) is $2^2 - 2^3 + 2^2(3) = 4 - 8 + 4(3) = 8$, which matches the target number. The correct answer is (E).

20. **A, B, C,** and **E**

Just start dividing to find the remainders. $117 \div 2 = 58$ with a remainder of 1, so select (A). 117 is divisible by 3, so 3 doesn't provide a remainder. $117 \div 4 = 29$ with a remainder of 1, which is still (A). $117 \div 5 = 23$ with a remainder of 2, so select (B). $117 \div 6 = 19$ with a remainder of 3, so select (C). $117 \div 7 = 16$ with a remainder of 5, so select (E). $117 \div 8 = 14$ with a remainder of 5, but (E) has already been selected. 117 is divisible by 9, so 9 doesn't give a remainder. The correct answer is (A), (B), (C), and (E).

NOTES

NOTES

NOTES

NOTES

International Offices Listing

China (Beijing)
1501 Building A,
Disanji Creative Zone,
No.66 West Section of North 4th Ring Road Beijing
Tel: +86-10-62684481/2/3
Email: tprkor01@chol.com
Website: www.tprbeijing.com

China (Shanghai)
1010 Kaixuan Road
Building B, 5/F
Changning District, Shanghai, China 200052
Sara Beattie, Owner: Email: sbeattie@sarabeattie.com
Tel: +86-21-5108-2798
Fax: +86-21-6386-1039
Website: www.princetonreviewshanghai.com

Hong Kong
5th Floor, Yardley Commercial Building
1-6 Connaught Road West, Sheung Wan, Hong Kong
(MTR Exit C)
Sara Beattie, Owner: Email: sbeattie@sarabeattie.com
Tel: +852-2507-9380
Fax: +852-2827-4630
Website: www.princetonreviewhk.com

India (Mumbai)
Score Plus Academy
Office No.15, Fifth Floor
Manek Mahal 90
Veer Nariman Road
Next to Hotel Ambassador
Churchgate, Mumbai 400020
Maharashtra, India
Ritu Kalwani: Email: director@score-plus.com
Tel: + 91 22 22846801 / 39 / 41
Website: www.score-plus.com

India (New Delhi)
South Extension
K-16, Upper Ground Floor
South Extension Part-1,
New Delhi-110049
Aradhana Mahna: aradhana@manyagroup.com
Monisha Banerjee: monisha@manyagroup.com
Ruchi Tomar: ruchi.tomar@manyagroup.com
Rishi Josan: Rishi.josan@manyagroup.com
Vishal Goswamy: vishal.goswamy@manyagroup.com
Tel: +91-11-64501603/ 4, +91-11-65028379
Website: www.manyagroup.com

Lebanon
463 Bliss Street
AlFarra Building - 2nd floor
Ras Beirut
Beirut, Lebanon
Hassan Coudsi: Email: hassan.coudsi@review.com
Tel: +961-1-367-688
Website: www.princetonreviewlebanon.com

Korea
945-25 Young Shin Building
25 Daechi-Dong, Kangnam-gu
Seoul, Korea 135-280
Yong-Hoon Lee: Email: TPRKor01@chollian.net
In-Woo Kim: Email: iwkim@tpr.co.kr
Tel: + 82-2-554-7762
Fax: +82-2-453-9466
Website: www.tpr.co.kr

Kuwait
ScorePlus Learning Center
Salmiyah Block 3, Street 2 Building 14
Post Box: 559, Zip 1306, Safat, Kuwait
Email: infokuwait@score-plus.com
Tel: +965-25-75-48-02 / 8
Fax: +965-25-75-46-02
Website: www.scorepluseducation.com

Malaysia
Sara Beattie MDC Sdn Bhd
Suites 18E & 18F
18th Floor
Gurney Tower, Persiaran Gurney
Penang, Malaysia
Email: tprkl.my@sarabeattie.com
Sara Beattie, Owner: Email: sbeattie@sarabeattie.com
Tel: +604-2104 333
Fax: +604-2104 330
Website: www.princetonreviewKL.com

Mexico
TPR México
Guanajuato No. 242 Piso 1 Interior 1
Col. Roma Norte
México D.F., C.P.06700
registro@princetonreviewmexico.com
Tel: +52-55-5255-4495
+52-55-5255-4440
+52-55-5255-4442
Website: www.princetonreviewmexico.com

Qatar
Score Plus
Office No: 1A, Al Kuwari (Damas)
Building near Merweb Hotel, Al Saad
Post Box: 2408, Doha, Qatar
Email: infoqatar@score-plus.com
Tel: +974 44 36 8580, +974 526 5032
Fax: +974 44 13 1995
Website: www.scorepluseducation.com

Taiwan
The Princeton Review Taiwan
2F, 169 Zhong Xiao East Road, Section 4
Taipei, Taiwan 10690
Lisa Bartle (Owner): lbartle@princetonreview.com.tw
Tel: +886-2-2751-1293
Fax: +886-2-2776-3201
Website: www.PrincetonReview.com.tw

Thailand
The Princeton Review Thailand
Sathorn Nakorn Tower, 28th floor
100 North Sathorn Road
Bangkok, Thailand 10500
Thavida Bijayendrayodhin (Chairman)
Email: thavida@princetonreviewthailand.com
Mitsara Bijayendrayodhin (Managing Director)
Email: mitsara@princetonreviewthailand.com
Tel: +662-636-6770
Fax: +662-636-6776
Website: www.princetonreviewthailand.com

Turkey
Yeni Sülün Sokak No. 28
Levent, Istanbul, 34330, Turkey
Nuri Ozgur: nuri@tprturkey.com
Rona Ozgur: rona@tprturkey.com
Iren Ozgur: iren@tprturkey.com
Tel: +90-212-324-4747
Fax: +90-212-324-3347
Website: www.tprturkey.com

UAE
Emirates Score Plus
Office No: 506, Fifth Floor
Sultan Business Center
Near Lamcy Plaza, 21 Oud Metha Road
Post Box: 44098, Dubai
United Arab Emirates
Hukumat Kalwani: skoreplus@gmail.com
Ritu Kalwani: director@score-plus.com
Email: info@score-plus.com
Tel: +971-4-334-0004
Fax: +971-4-334-0222
Website: www.princetonreviewuae.com

Our International Partners

The Princeton Review also runs courses with a variety of
partners in Africa, Asia, Europe, and South America.

Georgia
LEAF American-Georgian Education Center
www.leaf.ge

Mongolia
English Academy of Mongolia
www.nyescm.org

Nigeria
The Know Place
www.knowplace.com.ng

Panama
Academia Interamericana de Panama
http://aip.edu.pa/

Switzerland
Institut Le Rosey
http://www.rosey.ch/

All other inquiries, please email us at
internationalsupport@review.com